KENTUCKY TIMBER TOYS

ACKNOWLEDGEMENTS

This is the first, in which I hope will be many, toy books for woodworkers to build with. This has been quite a journey over the last 10 years, off an on as time permitted, as we have built many renditions of the toys that are now published in this book.

First and foremost, I want to thank my wife... she was the one who had to put up with me and my constant talk about this book. That she did so with love, patience and encouragement instead of putting a pillow over my face in the middle of the night says a great deal about her.

Next, I would not have completed this book without the assistance of my friend and neighbor John Miller. John stood by me in the garage at all hours, and helped cut out toy pieces, sanding and finishing prototypes, which ended up in the fire pit in the side yard and providing support until we had a solid toy that would stand up to the by-line: timber rough, timber tough.

I would like to also thank my family, business colleges and friends for also putting up with the constant talk and updates as new toys were developed, pictures were shared and allowing their children and grand children to play with them testing them for strength and durability.

With all of these folks supporting and encouraging me, and yes it sometimes takes a village, this book would not have been possible.

A huge thank you to all.

The Sandbox Series:

The Large Transportation:

Designed for the 3-year old's and up. These toys are the start of the interactive level for coupling and un-coupling trailers, hauling and maneuvering truck and trailer(s) in tandem. These toys include:

A Semi and a trailer(s) to be hauled behind it:

A Coal Mining truck:

A bulldozer:

Construction Vehicles:

Designed for 5-year-old and up. These toys are all interactive and rugged. They include:

A front -end loader:

An excavator:

A Fork Lift with palletized Cargo:

All the toys are designed to interact with each other with the thought of "as your child grows" so do the toys. There are 6 toys total in this series along with a specially designed Toy Box to hold all of the toys and also enhance your child's experience of having his or her own "walk in" toy store.

Contact us:

You can e-mail us at KentuckyTimberToys@gmail.com. We look forward to hearing from you and thank you for visiting our website. If there is something that you would like to see that is not on our website or have an idea for a wooden toy, please don't hesitate to contact us. We are always open to suggestions.

THE KENTUCKY TIMBER SEMI AND FLATBED TRAILER

The Semi and trailer that you are about to build is the all purpose "go to semi" in all of our designs. We have other semi designs but this one seems to be the most versatile in its use and coveted by the children. We made our Semi 14 inches long, 3 ½ inches wide and 8 inches tall. The flatbed trailer that we have paired with it is 19 inches long, 5 ½ inches wide and sits 3 inches tall.

Tools Recommended:

Drill / Drill Press	Sander/ Sand paper	White Wood Glue	Hammer / Mallet
3 /8, 9/32 and 1/4 Drill bits	1 ¼, 2" Dia Hole Saws	Jig Saw / Band saw	
(4) – 12" Clamps	¼" round over bit and router		

PAUL ARNOLD

Materials Needed:

A piece of Douglas Fir 3 ½ x 3 ½ x 9 (This will make parts A, and B, for the Semi)

A piece of 1 x 4 x 48 White Pine (This will make parts C, F, H, and L for the Semi and Parts A and B for the Trailer)

¾ Dowel Rod (comes in 48" lengths), this will make the main exhaust stacks. Parts J for the Semi

3/8 Dowel Rod (comes in 48" lengths), this will make the smaller parts of the exhaust. Parts K for the Semi and the trailer hitch pins, part K)

¼ Dowel Rod (comes in 48' lengths), This will make your Axles (part M and N for the Semi and part F for the Trailer)

The front bumper (part I) and the Gas tanks (part O) are odd pieces. You can use scrap out of the shop (if you have it) or you will need to buy a piece of poplar ¼ x 2 x 36 and a piece of 2 x 4 x 24 white pine for the semi and the trailer wheel hub spacer, part E for the trailer).

Sleeper Cab (Part L) is made out of a 2 x 6 x 11 white or yellow pine.

Layout:

So let's get started. First you will start by laying out the three (3) main parts of the *Semi* by:

(1) The Engine (part B), The Cab (part A), The sleeper cab (part L) and the wheel hubs (parts E & G)

(2) The Semi base (part C), The Front Fenders (part F), The Skid Plate (part H), and the wheels (parts L)

(3) The Main Exhaust (part J), the secondary exhaust (parts K) and the Gas Tanks (part O)

This will hopefully divide the tasks up in a common sense approach to the build and will save time and money.

The first layout that needs to be completed is a on a piece of 4 x 4 x 9 inch of Douglas Fir. We chose Douglas Fir for the color contrast, ease of shaping and sanding, cost containment and the finished appearance. When you get to the cutting and drilling phase it will be easier and safer to drill al your holes as indicated in the raw material prior to cutting them out. The larger block provides better stability and better clamping or hand hold surface then the small cut out pieces. The first step is to round over one end of the 4 x 4 Douglas Fir on the router with the ¼" round over bit. This will prevent tear out when you go to cut the space for the radiator. On the table saw, setting the fence ½ inch from the blade and running the piece on all four sides. You can use the router with a ¼ "bead bit and accomplish the same thing. It is your decision.

Then cut the "C" cab out with the 1 ¼ hole saw. This will not go all the way through the 4 x 4, so we finished it with the band saw as shown in picture. You could use a 1 ¼ "Forstner Bit and drill through, again your decision.

Make sure you read, understand and follow all of the safety instructions that come with your power tools.

When you are done with this phase you should have what is shown below.

The next layout will be of the Frame (part C), Fenders (part F), skid plate (part H) and the wheels (part L). This is made out of a single piece of 1 x 4 x 48-inch pine as indicated in the material listing.

Finally, the main exhaust and secondary exhaust tubes will need to be made from the ¾ dia and 3/8 dia dowel rod along with the Gas Tanks that are made out of a 2 x 2 x 5. Check the diagrams for the measurements and lay out. Cut out the remaining pieces (Wheel hubs, Wheels and the Sleeper Cab). These are not drawn out for you because they are straight forward cuts. Sleeper Cab is a 2x 6 (2 pieces) glued together and then squared. Final dimensions are on your cutting list. The pieces are shown below:

Make sure you read, understand and follow all of the safety instructions that come with your power tools.   3

We rounded over the tires just to take the edge off of them. You can accomplish this using sand paper or, as we did, use a 1' sander and a dowel rod to keep our fingers out of the belt.

Now that all the pieces are cut out, sanding all the rough edges and cleaning up the surfaces is the next step. This helps prevent any splintering and provides the finished product that the child will be playing with, a nice smooth surfaced edge. This can be accomplished by rounding over the edges with a ¼ " round over bit and routers or using a power sander or just good old fashion sandpaper and elbow grease. The choice is yours.

We are now ready to start assembly. You will need to start by gluing the main cab (part A) and the engine (part B) to the frame (part C). by gluing the parts together and clamped (as shown) you will ensure a tight bond between all of the parts.

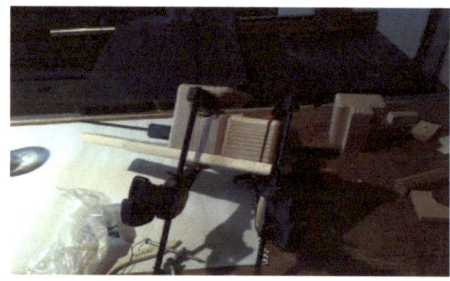 

It is very important that the sides of the cab and the engine block are flush with the chasse of the Semi. If they are not once you glue them together, sand them smooth with the belt sander and square them up.

Once that is complete glue the fenders into place. Now center and glue the Sleeper cab into place and set aside to dry.

Make sure you read, understand and follow all of the safety instructions that come with your power tools.

Then take the wheels (part E) and tap the Axles (Part M and N) into one of the wheels. This will be a press fit and no glue should be required. Slide the Wheel Hub (Part L) onto the other end of the Axil and tap the second wheel into place. Do the same with the rear wheels and then center and glue the wheel hubs into place. Congratulations you have completed the Semi portion of the build.

To make the trailer, cut the bed and bed top out of the 1 x 6 (part A and part B). You will then cut and inch off of part b and the angle the slope on the side (pictured below). We did this on the band saw. Then cut the corners off. These dimensions are found in the diagrams of the toy.

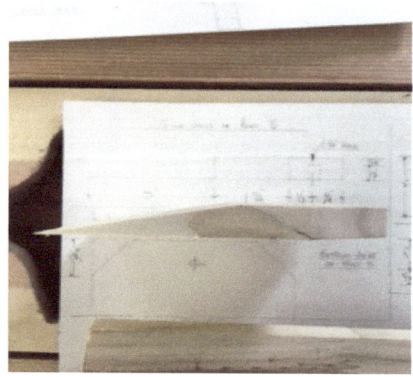 

Center the bed top on the bed. This will leave a ½ space on each side to assist in centering it. The 3" slop will set where the top sits and glue in place.

 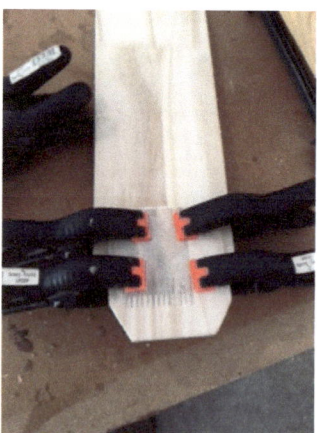

Now cut out part C (the rear wheel hub). Cut out the wheels (part D) and sand / round the edges as you did with the semi earlier.

Put the Wheels and Axles together (glue in between the wheel, part D and F) and you should have what is in pictured below.

Make sure you read, understand and follow all of the safety instructions that come with your power tools.

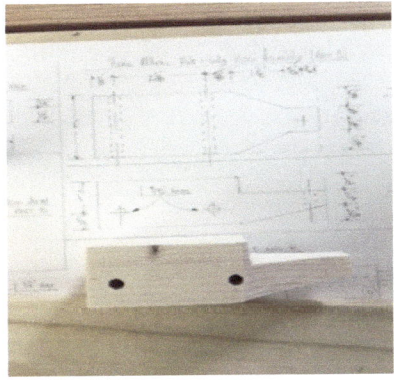
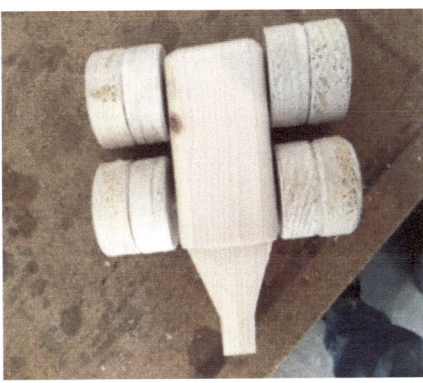

The reason for the extension on the rear wheel hub is there in case you want to add a dolly and hook up an additional trailer. Now center and drill a 3/8 inch hole in the bottom of the bed top (part B) and also in the extension of the real wheel hubs (part C) and insert the trailer hitch pins (part K).

Add the rear wheel hub spacer and glue in place (as shown on the placement diagram in your trailer plans).

Center the rear wheel assembly onto the trailer bed and glue into place. The trailer lift bar is the last item that needs to be made. Glue and clamp the assembly together, as indicated in the diagrams and then let it dry. Once dry, place the trailer lift bar assembly into place and glue.

Congratulations! You have now completed the trailer assembly. The finish is heavy duty exterior polyurethane to seal and preserve the wood allowing for the contrasting colors of the Douglas fir and pine to be brought out or you can chose to leave it unfinished and your child is afforded the opportunity to paint each toy his or her favorite color(s) making the toy his or her very own special one-of-a-kind possession. It also works well for Mom and Dad so that on days of inclimate weather, a project is at hand to keep little ones stimulated and engaged.

We do hope that you have enjoyed this project and found that the instructions and layout diagrams either met or exceeded your expectations. We look forward from hearing from you again with comments to help us improve, an additional purchase or both.

Make sure you read, understand and follow all of the safety instructions that come with your power tools.

THE KENTUCKY TIMBER SEMI AND FLATBED TRAILER

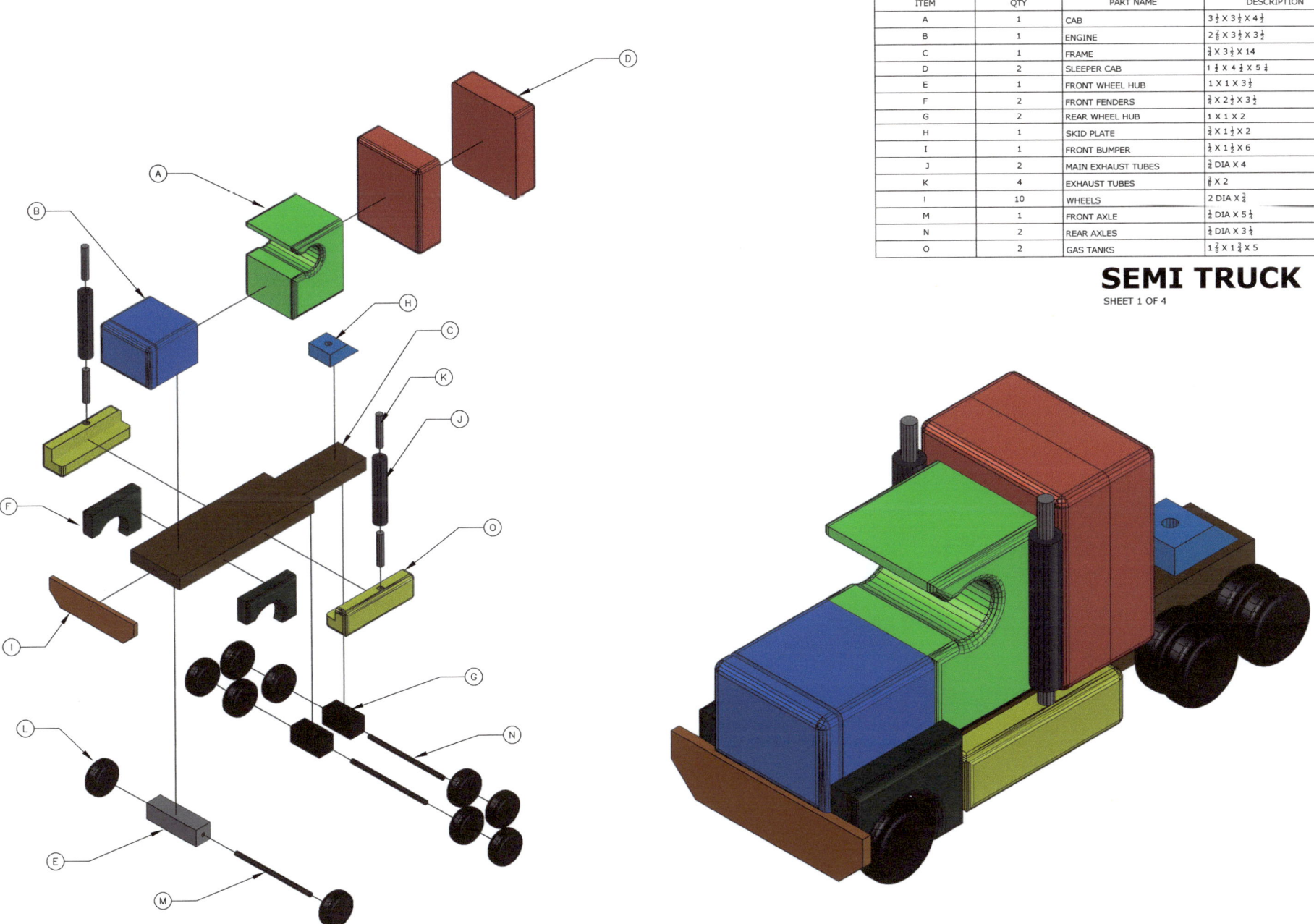

ITEM	QTY	PART NAME	DESCRIPTION
A	1	CAB	$3\frac{1}{2}$ X $3\frac{1}{2}$ X $4\frac{1}{2}$
B	1	ENGINE	$2\frac{7}{8}$ X $3\frac{1}{2}$ X $3\frac{1}{2}$
C	1	FRAME	$\frac{3}{4}$ X $3\frac{1}{2}$ X 14
D	2	SLEEPER CAB	$1\frac{1}{2}$ X $4\frac{1}{2}$ X $5\frac{1}{4}$
E	1	FRONT WHEEL HUB	1 X 1 X $3\frac{1}{2}$
F	2	FRONT FENDERS	$\frac{3}{4}$ X $2\frac{1}{2}$ X $3\frac{1}{2}$
G	2	REAR WHEEL HUB	1 X 1 X 2
H	1	SKID PLATE	$\frac{3}{4}$ X $1\frac{1}{2}$ X 2
I	1	FRONT BUMPER	$\frac{1}{2}$ X $1\frac{1}{2}$ X 6
J	2	MAIN EXHAUST TUBES	$\frac{3}{8}$ DIA X 4
K	4	EXHAUST TUBES	$\frac{3}{8}$ X 2
I	10	WHEELS	2 DIA X $\frac{3}{4}$
M	1	FRONT AXLE	$\frac{1}{4}$ DIA X $5\frac{1}{4}$
N	2	REAR AXLES	$\frac{1}{4}$ DIA X $3\frac{1}{4}$
O	2	GAS TANKS	$1\frac{7}{8}$ X $1\frac{3}{4}$ X 5

PARTS LIST

SEMI TRUCK

SHEET 1 OF 4

Make sure you read, understand and follow all of the safety instructions that come with your power tools.

9

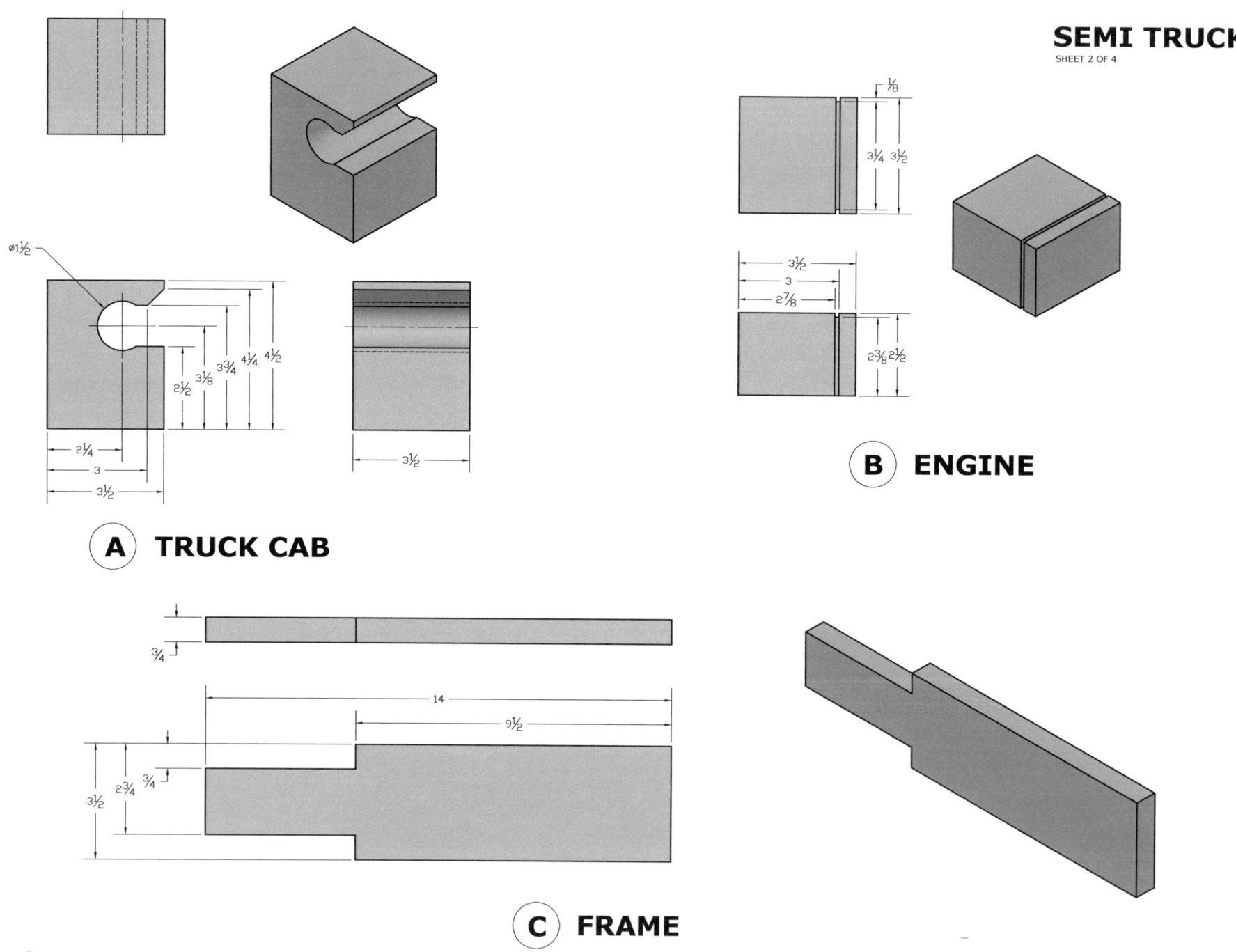

A TRUCK CAB

B ENGINE

C FRAME

Make sure you read, understand and follow all of the safety instructions that come with your power tools.

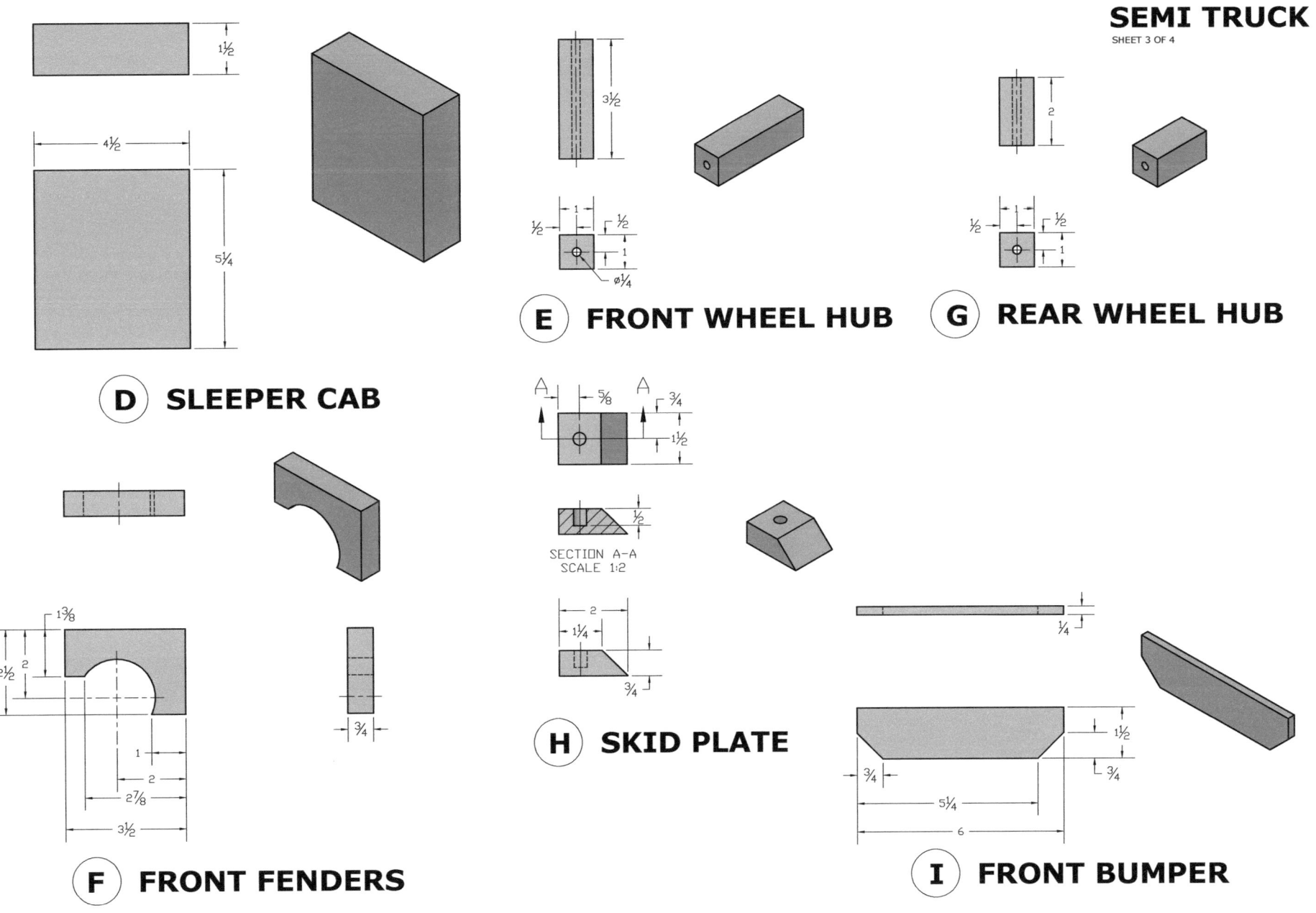

SEMI TRUCK
SHEET 3 OF 4

D) **SLEEPER CAB**

E) **FRONT WHEEL HUB**

G) **REAR WHEEL HUB**

H) **SKID PLATE**

F) **FRONT FENDERS**

I) **FRONT BUMPER**

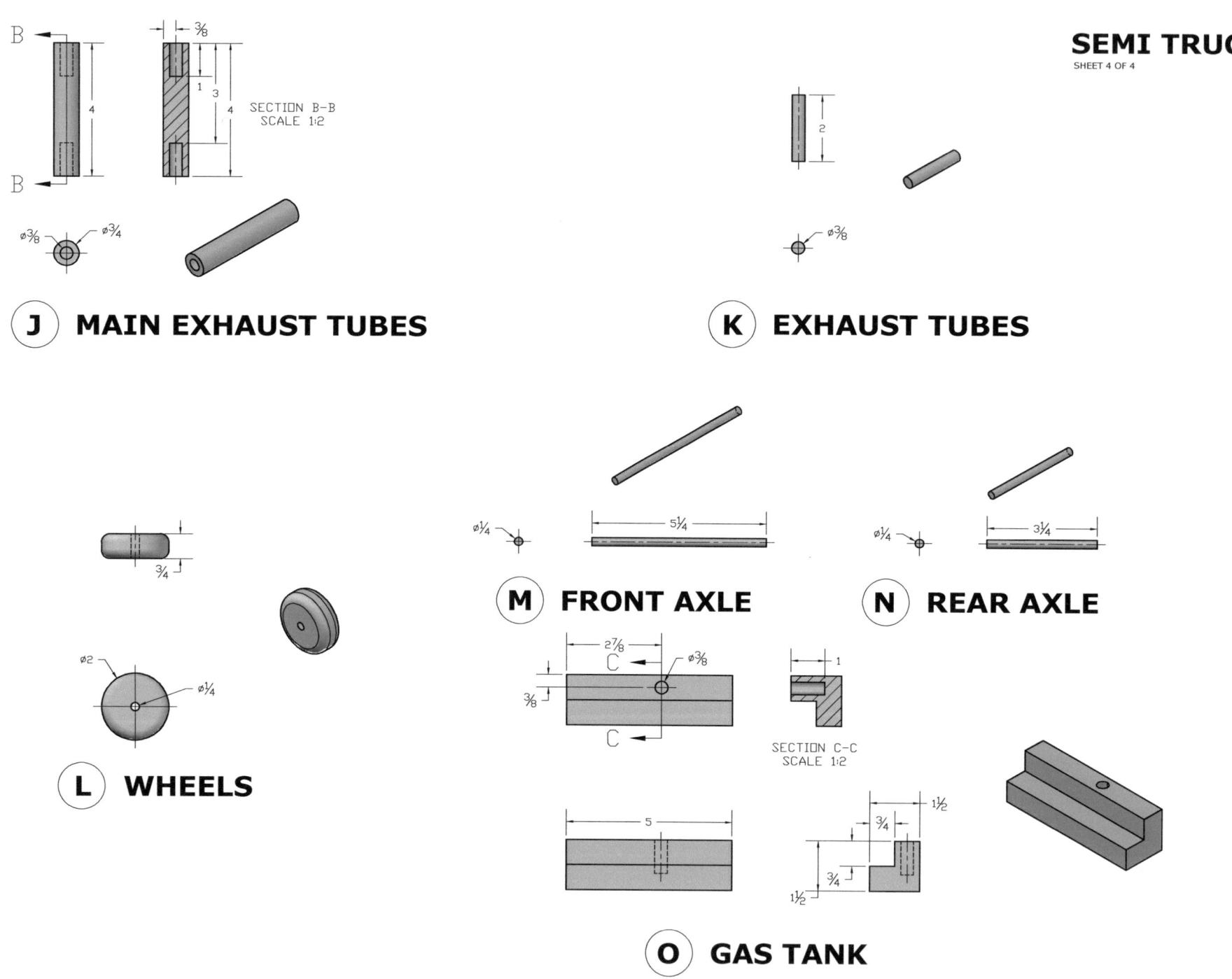

SECTION B-B
SCALE 1:2

(J) **MAIN EXHAUST TUBES**

(K) **EXHAUST TUBES**

(L) **WHEELS**

(M) **FRONT AXLE**

(N) **REAR AXLE**

SECTION C-C
SCALE 1:2

(O) **GAS TANK**

Make sure you read, understand and follow all of the safety instructions that come with your power tools.

KENTUCKY TIMBER TOYS

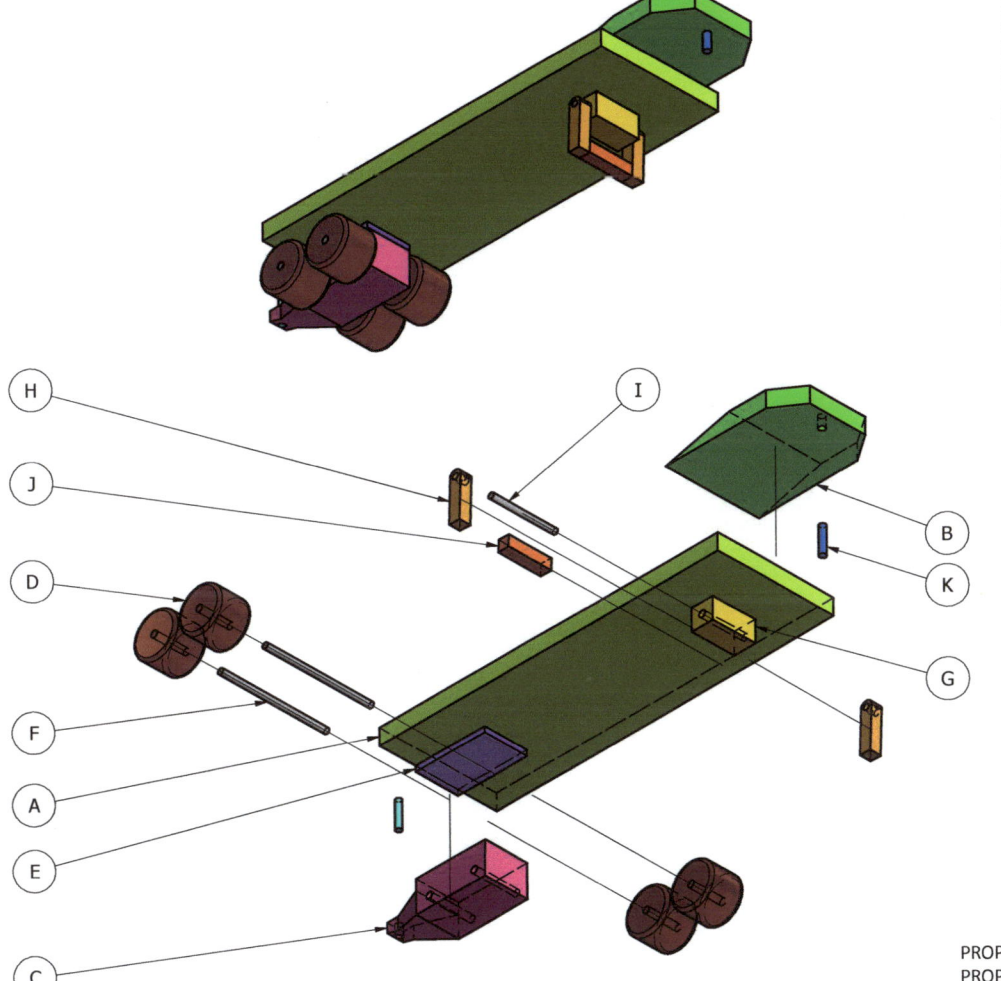

PARTS LIST			
ITEM	QTY	PART NUMBER	DESCRIPTION
A	1	BED	3/4 X 5 1/2 X 16
B	1	REAR TOP	3/4 X 4 1/4 X 6
C	1	REAR WHEEL HUB	1 1/2 X 2 X 5
D	8	WHEELS	2" DIA X 3/4
E	1	REAR WHEEL HUB SPACER	1/4 X 2 3 1/4
F	2	AXILS	1/4 DIA X 5 1/2
G	1	TRAILER LIFT BASE	1 X 1 X 2
H	2	TRAILER LIFT ARMS	1/2 X 1/2 X 2 1/4
I	1	TRAILER LIFT PIN	1/4 DIA X 3
J	1	TRAILER LIFT LOWER ARM	1/2 X 1/2 X 2
K	2	TRAILER HITCH PIN AND DOLLY PIN	1/4 DIA X 1 1/4

SEMI FLATBED TRAILER

SHEET 1 OF 4

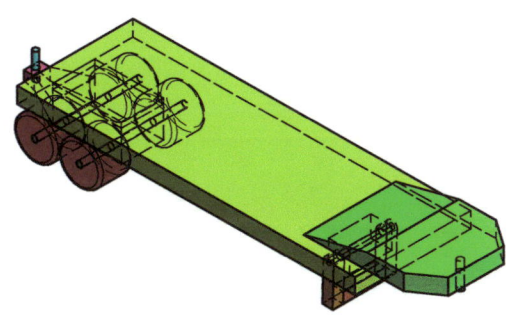

Make sure you read, understand and follow all of the safety instructions that come with your power tools.

PAUL ARNOLD

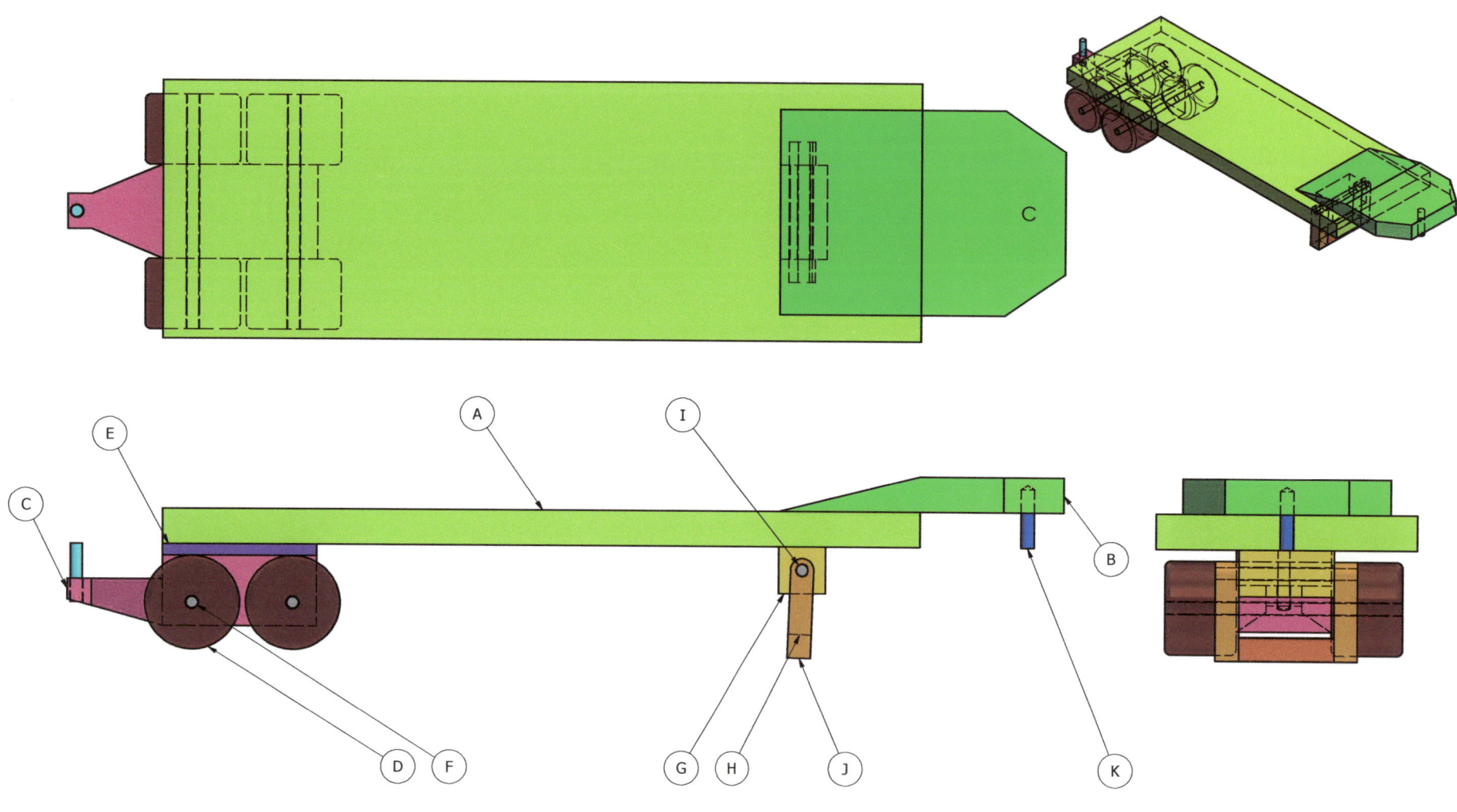

Make sure you read, understand and follow all of the safety instructions that come with your power tools.

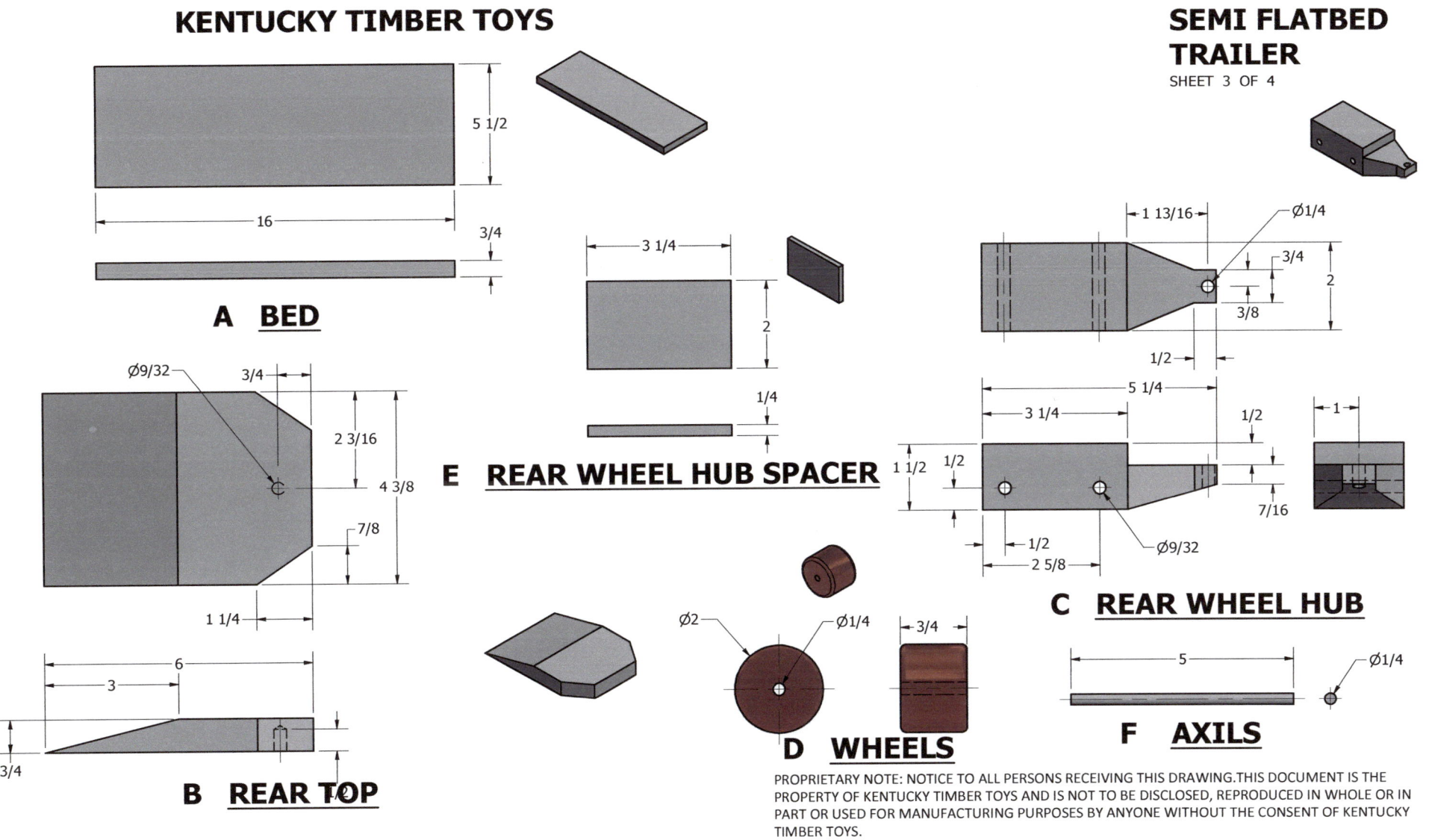

KENTUCKY TIMBER TOYS

SEMI FLATBED TRAILER

SHEET 3 OF 4

A **BED**

5 1/2

16

3/4

B **REAR TOP**

Ø9/32

3/4

2 3/16

4 3/8

7/8

1 1/4

6

3

3/4

E **REAR WHEEL HUB SPACER**

3 1/4

2

1/4

D **WHEELS**

Ø2

Ø1/4

3/4

C **REAR WHEEL HUB**

1 13/16

Ø1/4

3/4

2

3/8

1/2

5 1/4

3 1/4

1/2

1

1 1/2

1/2

7/16

1/2

2 5/8

Ø9/32

F **AXILS**

5

Ø1/4

Make sure you read, understand and follow all of the safety instructions that come with your power tools.

KENTUCKY TIMBER TOYS

SEMI FLATBED TRAILER
SHEET 4 OF 4

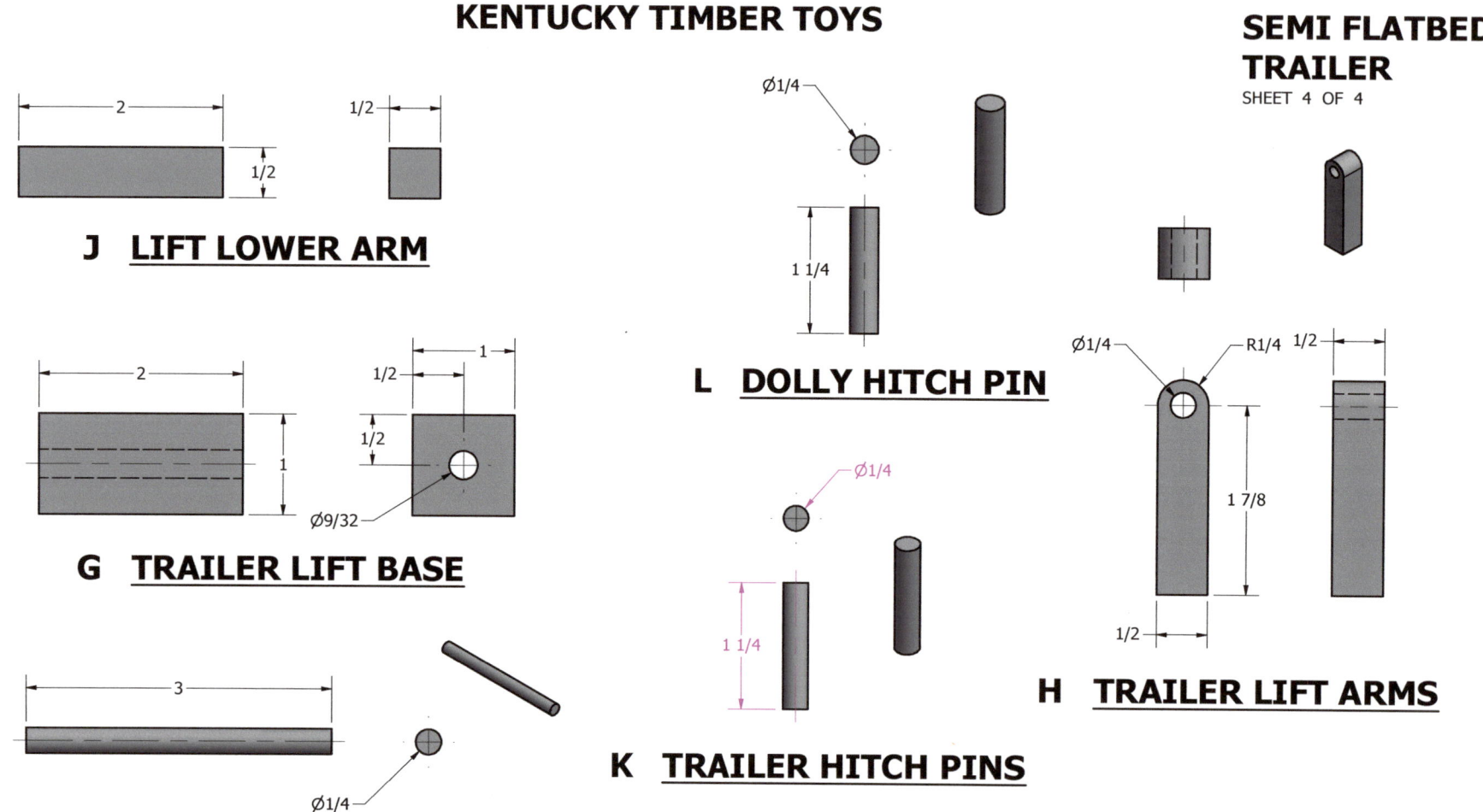

J   LIFT LOWER ARM

G   TRAILER LIFT BASE

L   DOLLY HITCH PIN

K   TRAILER HITCH PINS

H   TRAILER LIFT ARMS

I   TRAILER LIFT PIN

Make sure you read, understand and follow all of the safety instructions that come with your power tools.

THE KENTUCKY COAL TRUCK

The Coal Truck design was brought about wanting to have a dump truck in the construction line of toys but at the same time to have a symbol of Kentucky. With over 94 percent of Kentucky's electricity coming from coal generated power plants and Kentucky being third in the nation in coal production, we thought it was an appropriate piece to be in our construction set.

Recommended Tools Needed:

Drill press	2" Drum Sander	1" belt Sander	White Wood Glue
Hammer / Mallet	9/32 and 3/8 Drills	3" Dia Hole Saw	Band saw
2 – 6" Bar Clamps	4- 2" spring clamps	¼ "round over bit and router	Table Saw
Flush trim saw	1" hole saw		

Materials Needed:

A piece of ½ x 5 ½ x 36 (comes in 3 ft lengths) poplar. The entire bed can be made out of 30".

A piece of ¼ x 5 ½ x 36 (comes in 3 ft lengths) poplar

A piece of Yellow Pine that is 1 ½ " x 10 x 16 ½ (we used a piece of 2 x 10 x 16 ½)

A piece of Douglas Fir that is 3 ½ x 3 ½ x 9 (basic 4 x 4 x 9)

An 1 ¼ inch diameter wooden ball (you can pick this up at any craft shop)

A piece of ¼ dowel rod (comes in 48" length) double check the drill bit in your hole saw mandrel, it should be 1 size smaller than ¼" . this way the axils will press fit into the large 3" wheels.

A piece of 3/8 dia Dowel Rod (come in 48" length)

A bottle of wood glue (we use Gorilla wood glue)

Layout and cutting:

First you will start by laying out the Body (A). The first thing is to run the best end piece that you see on all four faces through the router with a ¼ round over bit. This will prevent later splitting of the wood when you complete the next step. Then on the table saw, set the fence ½ from the blade and the blade to ¼ inch deep. Then run the body through on all four sides to create the grill of the truck. Another option s to use a router with a ¼ inch bead bit and run it around the face of the 4 x 4. It is your decision on what you are comfortable with. It is best if you drill the holes for the wheel axles now while the body is still in one piece. (Parts O and P). Then, on the band saw cut out the back half of the truck. Start with the side cut first, they are straight and will be easy to complete first. At this time take some tape and wrap it around the two sides and hold them in place so you can cut the dump bar and back strap out.

Make sure you read, understand and follow all of the safety instructions that come with your power tools.

Next you will need to cut out the wheels, Once the wheels are cut out you will want to router them and the front two fenders prior to cutting them free. Lay out the front fenders around two of the wheels so that you can router them in a large block of wood and maintain the curve of the wheel. We used a ¼ dowel rod to round over the wheels so that our hands were kept away from the router bit.

  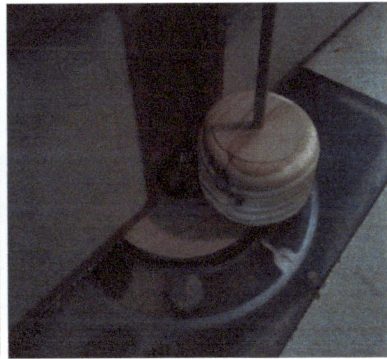

The last section to layout and cut is the dump bed. Layout everything in pieces and cut them out. We used a band saw for ease and precision. You can use a jig saw; however, you will need to be very careful and clamp everything down so that it does not move around. The cutting out of the dump bed parts is pretty straight forward. We cut them just outside of the lines and then with a small 1" belt sander brought it down to the lines as indicated in the drawings. When drilling the 3/8-inch hole in part J (the dump bed tabs), tape the two tabs together and mark out the hole and drill it at one time. This will ensure that placement is correct. Now that all the pieces are cut out, sanding all the rough edges. This helps prevent any splintering and provides the finished product that the child will be playing with, a nice smooth surfaced edge. This can be accomplished by using a power sander or just good old fashion sandpaper and elbow grease.

We are now ready to start assembly. You will need to start by gluing the Cab together. Then the engine base (D) and exhaust (E) need to be glued together. While those pieces are drying, glue the dump bed bar (B) to the rear of the body (center the bar on the body cut out). Then glue the wheels (M) and axils (O and P) in place.

Once dry glue the cab base (C) and then the engine base and exhaust into place. Make sure all the parts (C, D, E and L) line up behind the radiator so that it shows prominently on the toy. Notice that there is a 1/16" setback of the Cab and the Engine exhaust.

Cut out the cab as shown in the diagram of part F in the plans, sand to your preference and glue in place. Glue the front fenders (L) into place. Your toy should look like the picture below at this time.

The dump bed is glued together by edge gluing all the parts and then clamping them together. Start with the Bed (part G) of the dump laying flat and then the two sides (part I) fit against the sides of the bed. The front (part H) sits on top of the bed bottom and inside the two sides. Clamp as needed to ensure they are solid and square.

Make sure you read, understand and follow all of the safety instructions that come with your power tools.

Cut the interactive arm as shown and then drill the interactive ball. When you round the interactive arm you want to keep it as close to the ½ inch as possible. We used the 1" belt sander to complete this. You can use a hand rasp to round the end of the interactive arm, however, you need to continuously check the fit as you take material off the interactive arm.

Once dried, we sanded all the joints to ensure a square bed and then glued the top on. You will have to sand the dump bed front (part H) at an angle that matches the two sides so that the top Part Q)will sit flat on all three pieces.

The first 1 ½ of the top sits on the sides and the front to ensure a strong and secure base for the interactive arm and ball so it pulls freely and does not bind (pictured below).

We found it easier to place the dump bed pin (R) in place and then the tabs (J) in place and glue them prior to mounting the bed.

This allowed us to make sure that the bed was square on the toy even if the dump bar hole was off a little. Once dried, Square and glue the bed onto the tabs.

Now that the tabs are dry, mark the positions of them with a square in the top of the dump bed and fined their centers. Use a Dremel tool with a ¼ inch bit and drill 4 holes (two in each tab) as shown on your parts drawing, glue and tap in the dowel pins and let dry. Trim with a flush trim saw and sand smooth. This will enhance the strength of the tabs to the bed of the dump. This will bring you to the end of the project.

Make sure you read, understand and follow all of the safety instructions that come with your power tools.

KENTUCKY TIMBER TOYS

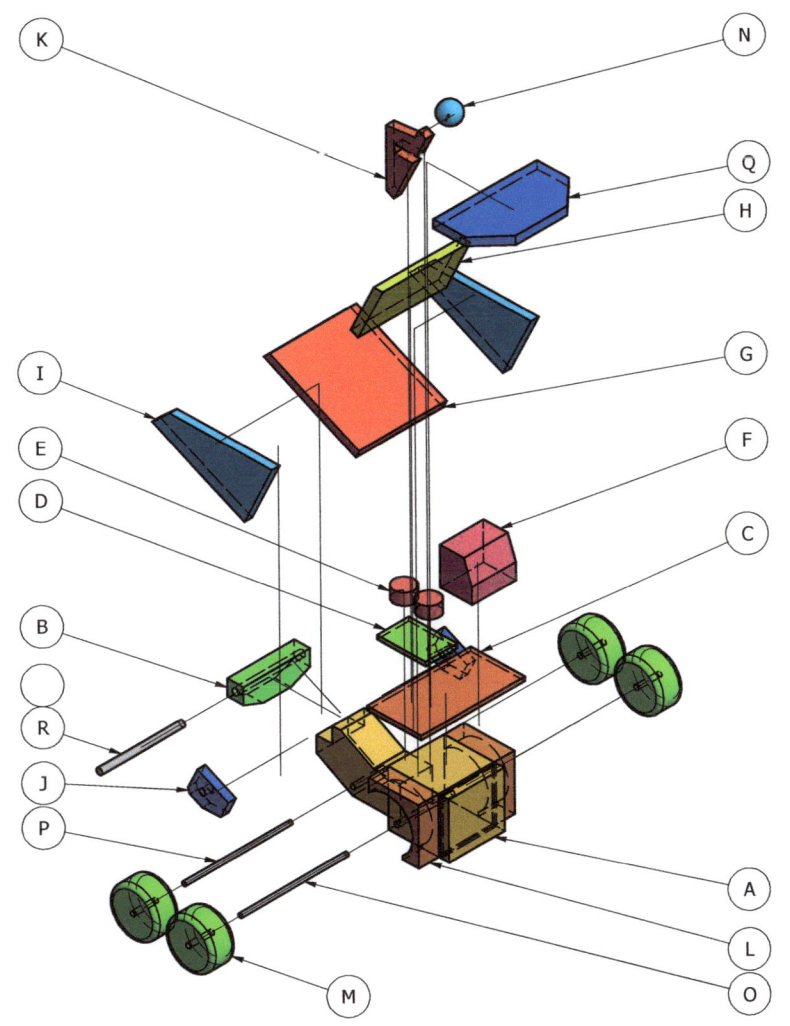

PARTS LIST			
ITEM	QTY	PART NUMBER	DESCRIPTION
A	1	BODY	3 1/2 X 3 1/2 X 9
B	1	REAR DUMP BAR	1 1/2 X 1 X 4 1/4
C	1	CAB BASE	1/4 X 3 3/8 X 6 1/2
D	1	ENGINE BASE	1/4 X 3 X 2
E	2	ENGINE EXHAUST	1 1/4 DIA X 3/4
F	1	CAB	2 X 2 3/8 X 2 3/4
G	1	DUMP BED BOTTOM	1/2 X 5 1/2 X 6 1/2
H	1	DUMP BED FRONT	1/2 X 3 3/4 X 5 1/2
I	2	DUMP BED SIDES	1/2 X 5 1/2 X 6 3/8
J	2	DUMP BED TABS	1/2 X 1 3/4 X 2
K	1	INTERACTIVE ARM	1/2 X 2 X 5
L	2	FRONT WHEEL FENDERS	1 1/2 X 3 1/8 X 3 1/2
M	6	WHEELS	1 1/2 X 3 DIA
N	1	INTERACTIVE BALL	1 1/4 DIA
O	1	FRONT AXIL	1/4 DIA X 6 1/2
P	1	REAR AXIL	1/4 DIA X 7 5/8
Q	1	DUMP BED TOP	1/2 X 3 2/1 X 6 1/2
	1	DUMP BED PIN	3/8 DIA X 5 1/4

COAL TRUCK

SHEET 1 OF 4

Make sure you read, understand and follow all of the safety instructions that come with your power tools.

KENTUCKY TIMBER TOYS

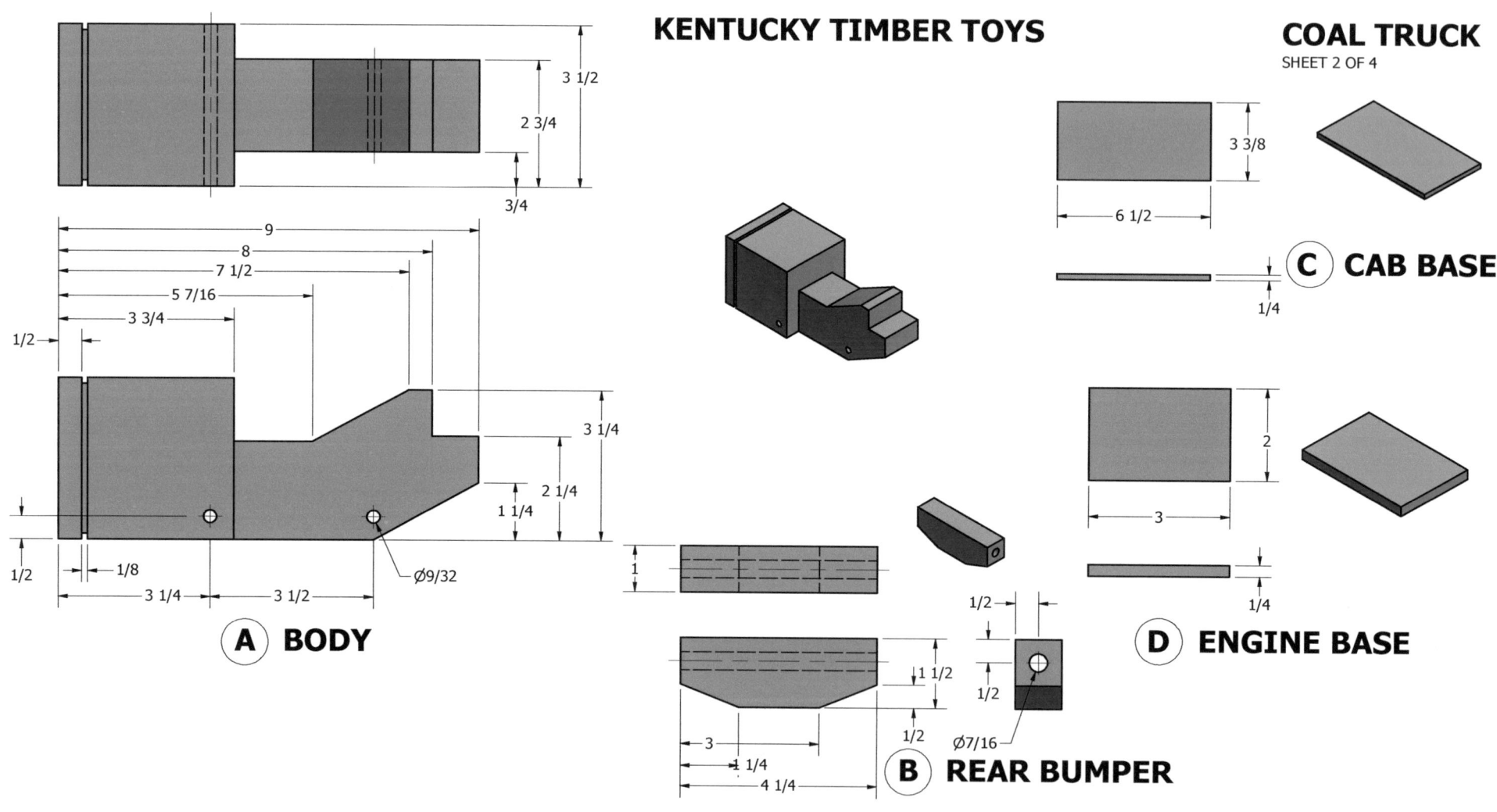

3 1/2

2 3/4

3/4

9

8

7 1/2

5 7/16

3 3/4

1/2

3 1/4

3 1/4

2 1/4

1 1/4

1/2

1/8

Ø9/32

3 1/4

3 1/2

A BODY

3 3/8

6 1/2

C CAB BASE

1/4

2

3

1/4

D ENGINE BASE

1

1/2

1 1/2

1/2

1/2

3

1 1/4

4 1/4

Ø7/16

B REAR BUMPER

PROPRIETARY NOTE: NOTICE TO ALL PERSONS RECEIVING THIS DRAWING.THIS DOCUMENT IS THE PROPERTY OF KENTUCKY TIMBER TOYS AND IS NOT TO BE DISCLOSED, REPRODUCED IN WHOLE OR IN PART OR USED FOR MANUFACTURING PURPOSES BY ANYONE WITHOUT THE CONSENT OF KENTUCKY TIMBER TOYS.

Make sure you read, understand and follow all of the safety instructions that come with your power tools.

KENTUCKY TIMBER TOYS

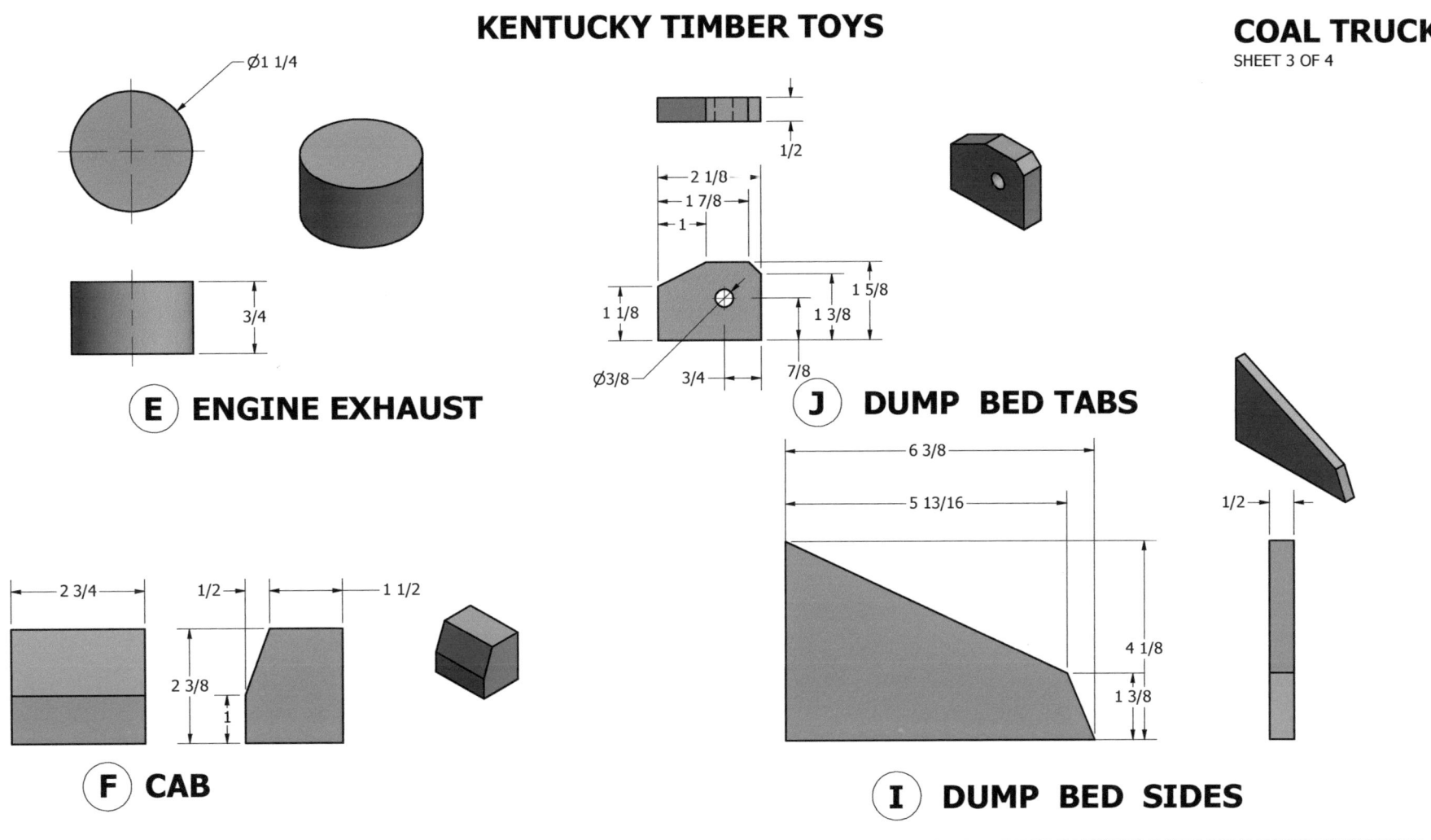

Ø1 1/4

3/4

E **ENGINE EXHAUST**

1/2

2 1/8
1 7/8
1

1 1/8

1 5/8
1 3/8
Ø3/8   3/4   7/8

J **DUMP BED TABS**

6 3/8

5 13/16

4 1/8

1 3/8

1/2

I **DUMP BED SIDES**

2 3/4   1/2   1 1/2

2 3/8
1

F **CAB**

Make sure you read, understand and follow all of the safety instructions that come with your power tools.

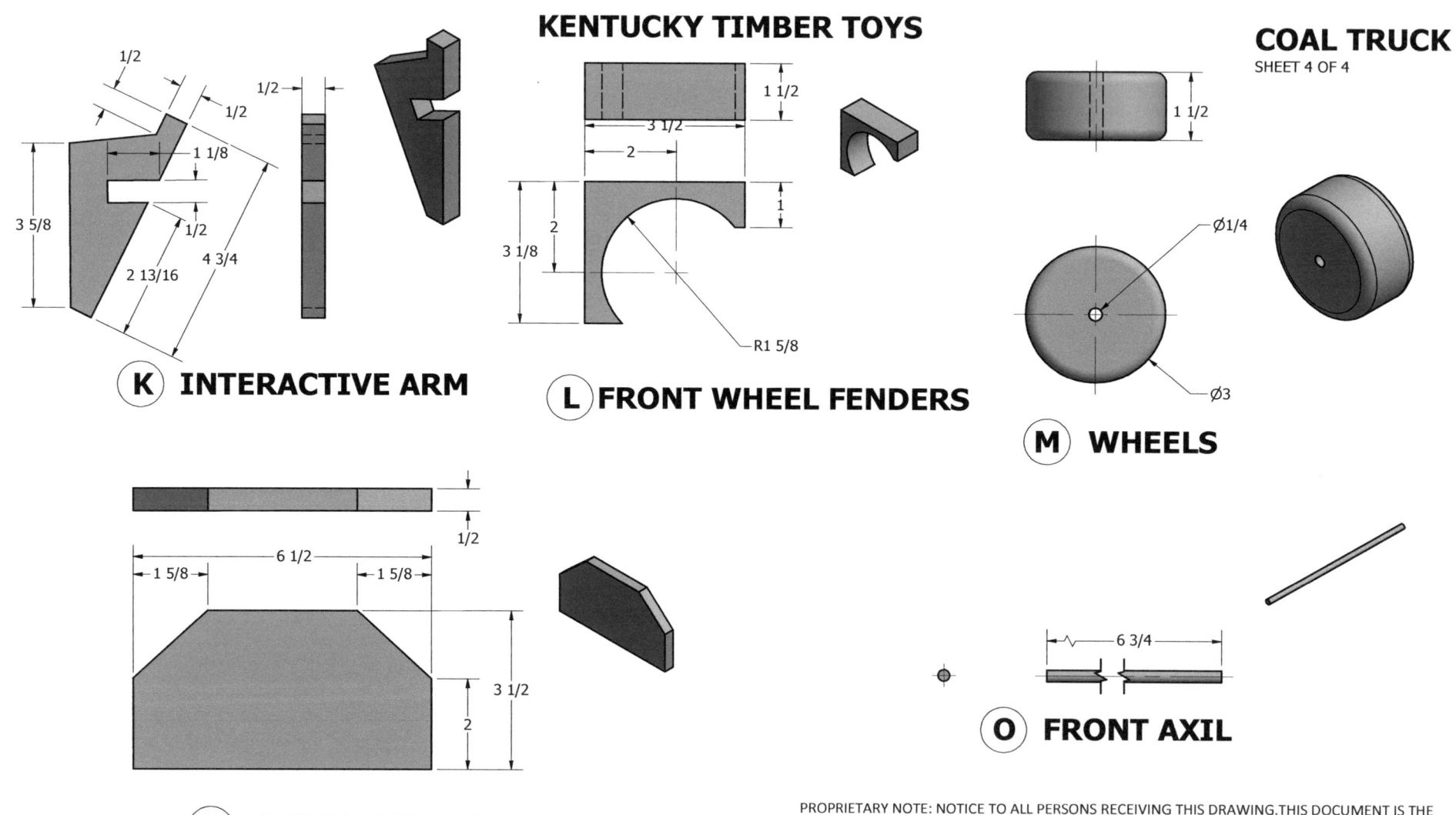

KENTUCKY TIMBER TOYS

COAL TRUCK
SHEET 4 OF 4

(K) INTERACTIVE ARM

(L) FRONT WHEEL FENDERS

(M) WHEELS

(Q) DUMP BED TOP

(O) FRONT AXIL

Make sure you read, understand and follow all of the safety instructions that come with your power tools.

THE KENTUCKY TIMBER DOZER

We made ours 14 inches long and 6 ½ inches wide and it works with all the toys in the Construction set that we have developed. It started out being a hand eye coordination development toy by using the interactive ball to raise and lower the blade. We chopped and dropped it to give it some style and the C bad design was to keep little fingers out from under the wheels.

Tools Recommended:

Drill / Drill Press	Sander/ Sand paper	White Wood Glue	Hammer / Mallet
3 /8, 9/32 and 1/4 Drill bits	1 ¼, 2, 2 ½ and a 3" Dia Hole Saws	Jig Saw / Band saw	
(4) – 6" Clamps	¼" round over bit and router	A Dremel tool	

Materials Needed:

A piece of Douglas Fir 3 ½ x 3 ½ x 12 (This will make parts A, B, C, D and Q)

A piece of 2 x 4 x 24 white Pine (this will make parts E, F, G and H)

A piece of 1 x 4 x 12 White Pine (This will make parts I)

¼ Dowel Rod (comes in 48" lengths), this will make parts R and S

A piece of ½ x 5 ½ x 48 Poplar / pine (this will make parts J, M, N and O)

1 ¼ Día Wooden Ball (this can be purchased at any hobby shop, part P)

¾ Día Wooden Dowel (makes part K)

3/8 Día wooden dowel (makes part L)

Layout

The build is done in three phases. The body, the wheels and fenders and finally the front support arms and the blade assembly. Draw out the Body (part A), Cab (part B), the lower engine block (part C), the Hood (part D and the upper engine block (Part Q). We chose Douglas Fir for the color contrast, ease of shaping and sanding, cost containment and the finished appearance. When you get to cutting and drilling the parts it will be easier and safer to drill all your holes as indicated in the material prior to cutting them out. The larger block provides better stability and better clamping or hand hold surface area than the small cut out pieces. Now, drill your 1 ¼ inch Cab hole and the three 9/32 holes for your wheel hubs.

Once your holes are drilled, Use the 1 ¼ with the hole saw to cut the shape of the "C" cab. The hole saw will not go all the way through. You will need to cut it out with the band saw or use a 1 ¼ "Forstner Bit to drill all the way through. Finish cutting out all the other parts from the block and you should have what is shown below.

Make sure you read, understand and follow all of the safety instructions that come with your power tools.

Drill the wheels out of the 2 x 4 (parts F, G, and H) and then cut out the fenders (part E) as shown on the plans. _Remember you have a right and left fender. They need to be mirrors of each other._ Repeat this process so that you have two fenders and six wheels.

Now sand all the parts to your preference. We routered all the parts to take all the sharp edges off the parts. We only routered one side of each fender (parts E) so that the surface that is glued to the body is flat and provides the best adhesion. This will complete phase 1 and 2 of the build. Begin assembling what you have done by gluing the body (parts A, B, C, D and Q) together and clamp them to dry. The lower engine block (Part C) needs to be centered on the front part of the Body (Part A).

Make sure you read, understand and follow all of the safety instructions that come with your power tools.

While this is drying, make you muffler with parts N and O. Take the muffler (part O) and drill a 13/32-inch hole through the part. Slide the Muffler pipe (part N) through the hole and glue in place. You will want a ¼ inch exposed on the top of the muffler, then place into the muffler hole in the body (part A) that you drilled in the beginning. Space the muffler assembly a little shorter than the cab. This will make sure that does not get broken off or someone falls onto a sharp object. You will now drill the 9/32 hole in the lower engine block (part C) to accept the dozer arms (part I) and the dozer pin (part S). Lay the dozer arm (part I) onto the space created between the body (Part A) and the engine hood (part D). This will level the Dozer Arm to the Body. The Dozer arm should have a ¼" space between the arm drop and the front of the body. This will center the hole at ½" from the rear of the lower engine block. Mark and drill the hole through the lower engine block. Tap the Axles into one side of the wheels and then slide them through the proper holes on the body. Then tap the second wheel into place. Now that you have all of this together, set aside to dry. Attach the arms and place the pin into place. Complete the arms and pin assembly prior to gluing the fenders into place. Once the arms are in place now you can glue the fenders (part E) into place. We set one side on at a time to get placement correct.

Once both were somewhat dry, we placed blocks on both sides and then tightened the clamps to ensure a good adhesion process.

Place the lower blade and upper blade (part M and part N) together and glue. Then glue the sides (part J) and clamp. When they are dry, sand into the final shape that you want.

Make sure you read, understand and follow all of the safety instructions that come with your power tools.

Cut out the interactive arm per the drawings on page 4 (part O) and drill your ½ inch hole in the interacitve ball. Round over the ½ end of the interactive arm, we did it on a 1" belt sander, and glue the ball into place.

Now glue the arm onto the center of the blade. Once dry glue the blade and arm assembly to the dozer arms and let dry. After this was dry, take a Dremel tool and drill four ¼ inch holes through the blade into the center of the dozer arms and tapped ¼ inch dowels (Part S) into place with glue. This was to increase the strength of the blade and secure the attached joint. Congratulations you have finished the build.

KENTUCKY TIMBER TOYS

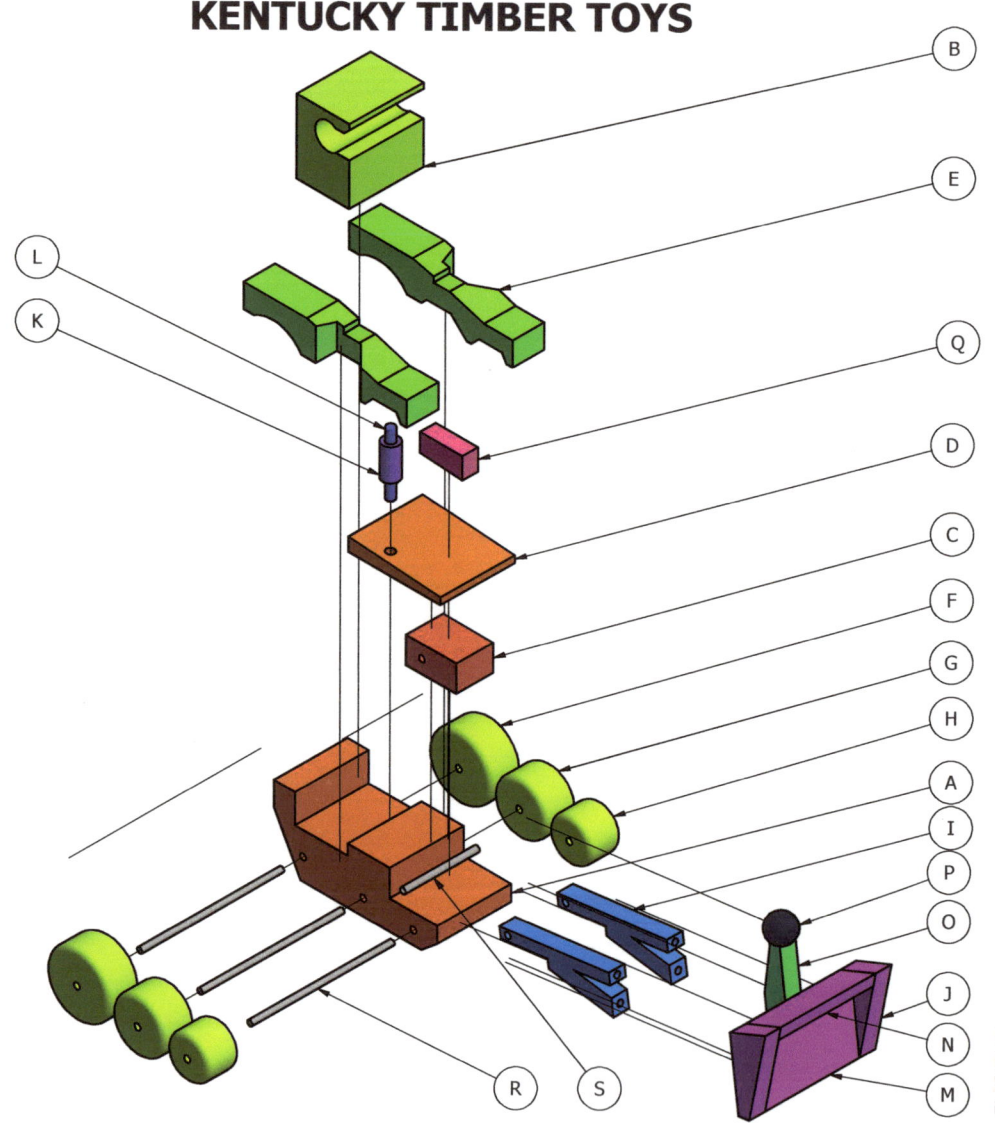

PARTS LIST			
ITEM	QTY	PART NUMBER	DESCRIPTION
A	1	BODY	3 1/2 X 3 1/2 X 8
B	1	CAB	2 1/2 X 3 1/2 X 3 1/2
C	1	LOWER ENGINE BLOCK	1 1/4 X 2 X 2 1/2
D	1	HOOD	7/8 X 3 1/2 X 4 1/8
E	2	FENDERS	1 1/2 X 2 1/2 X 8 1/4
F	2	REAR WHEELS	3 DIA X 1 1/2
G	2	CENTER WHEELS	2 1/2 DIA X 1 1/2
H	2	FRONT WHEELS	2 DIA X 1 1/2
I	2	DOZER ARMS	3/4 X 2 3/4 X 5 1/2
J	2	BLADE SIDES	1/2 X 1 3/4 X 3 3/4
K	1	MUFFLER	3/4 DIA X 1 1/2
L	1	MUFFLER PIPE	3/8 DIA X 2
M	1	BLADE	1/2 X 3 1/2 X 5 1/2
N	1	BLADE TOP	1/2 X 1 1/2 X 5 1/2
O	1	INTERACTIVE ARM	1/2 X 3/4 X 5 1/4
P	1	INTERACTIVE BALL	1 1/4 DIA WOODEN BALL
Q	1	UPPER ENGINE BLOCK	3/4 X 2 X 2
R	3	AXILS	1/4 DIA X 6 1/2
S	1	DOZER ARMS PIN	1/4 DIA X 3 1/2

DOZER
SHEET 1 OF 9

Make sure you read, understand and follow all of the safety instructions that come with your power tools.

KENTUCKY TIMBER TOYS

DOZER

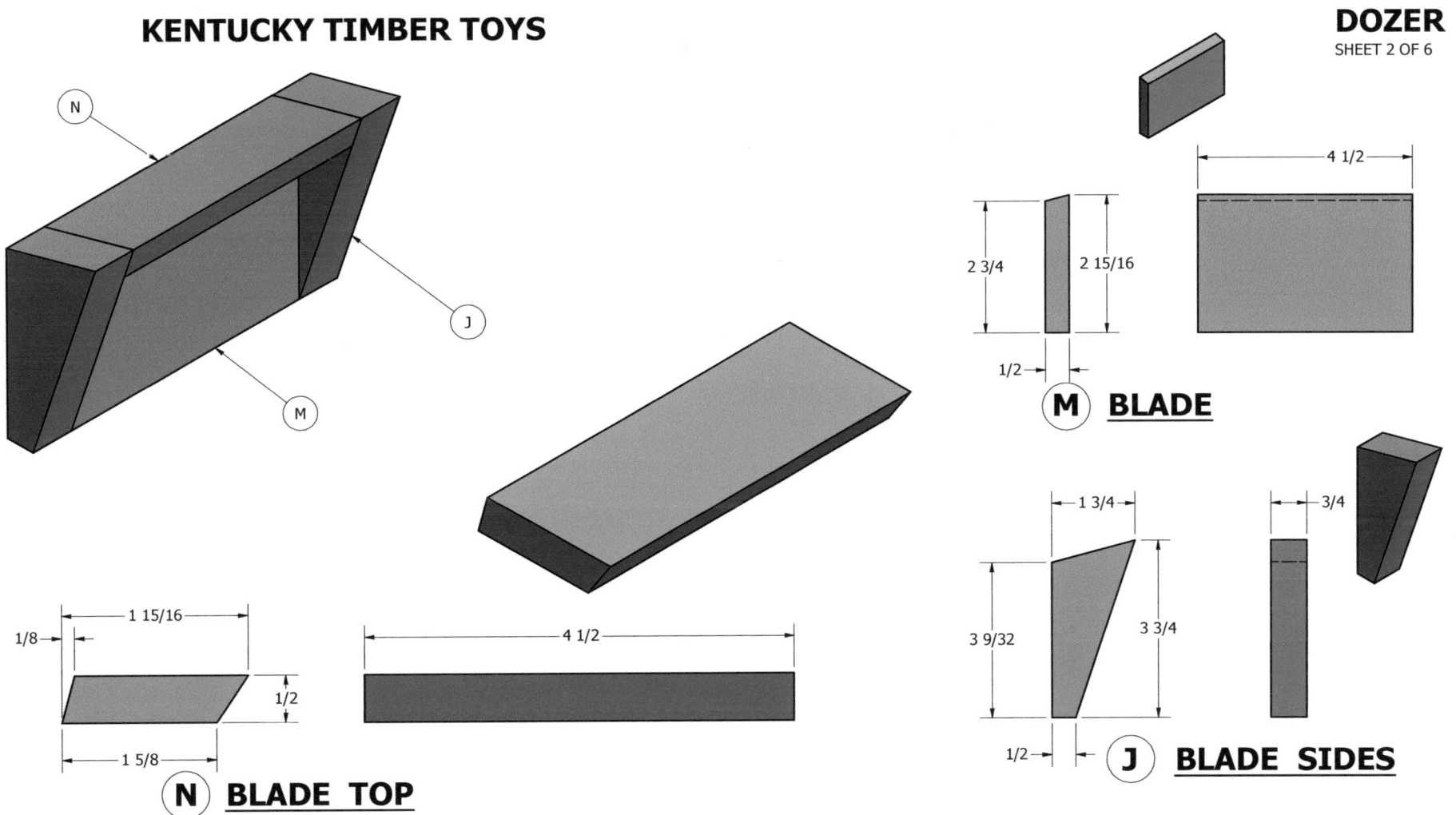

4 1/2

2 3/4   2 15/16

1/2

M BLADE

1 3/4   3/4

3 9/32   3 3/4

1/2   **J** BLADE SIDES

1 15/16
1/8
1/2
1 5/8
N BLADE TOP

4 1/2

KENTUCKY TIMBER TOYS

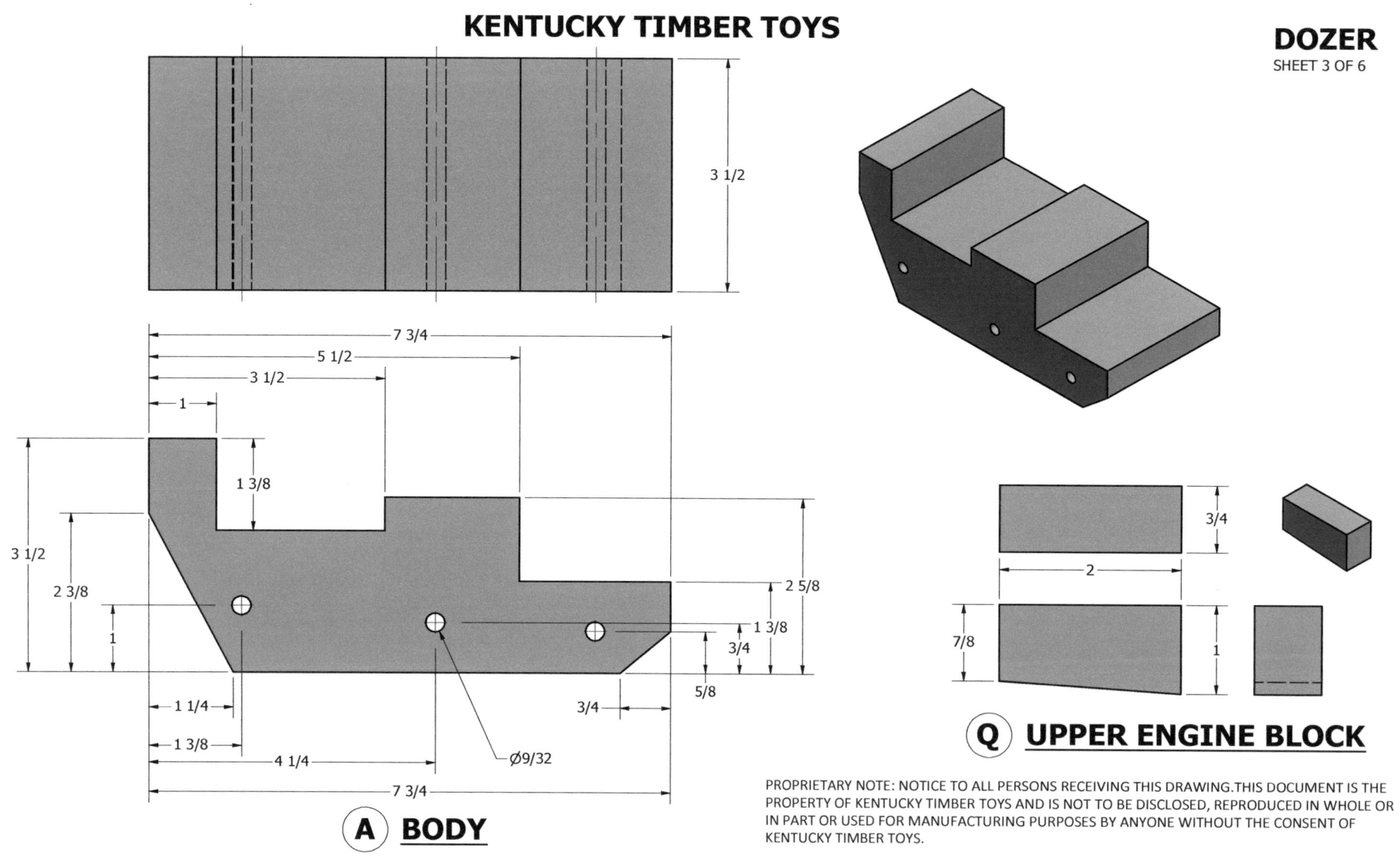

3 1/2

7 3/4

5 1/2

3 1/2

1

1 3/8

3 1/2

2 3/8

1

2 5/8

1 3/8

3/4

5/8

1 1/4

3/4

1 3/8

4 1/4

Ø9/32

7 3/4

(A) BODY

3/4

2

7/8

1

(Q) UPPER ENGINE BLOCK

Make sure you read, understand and follow all of the safety instructions that come with your power tools.

KENTUCKY TIMBER TOYS

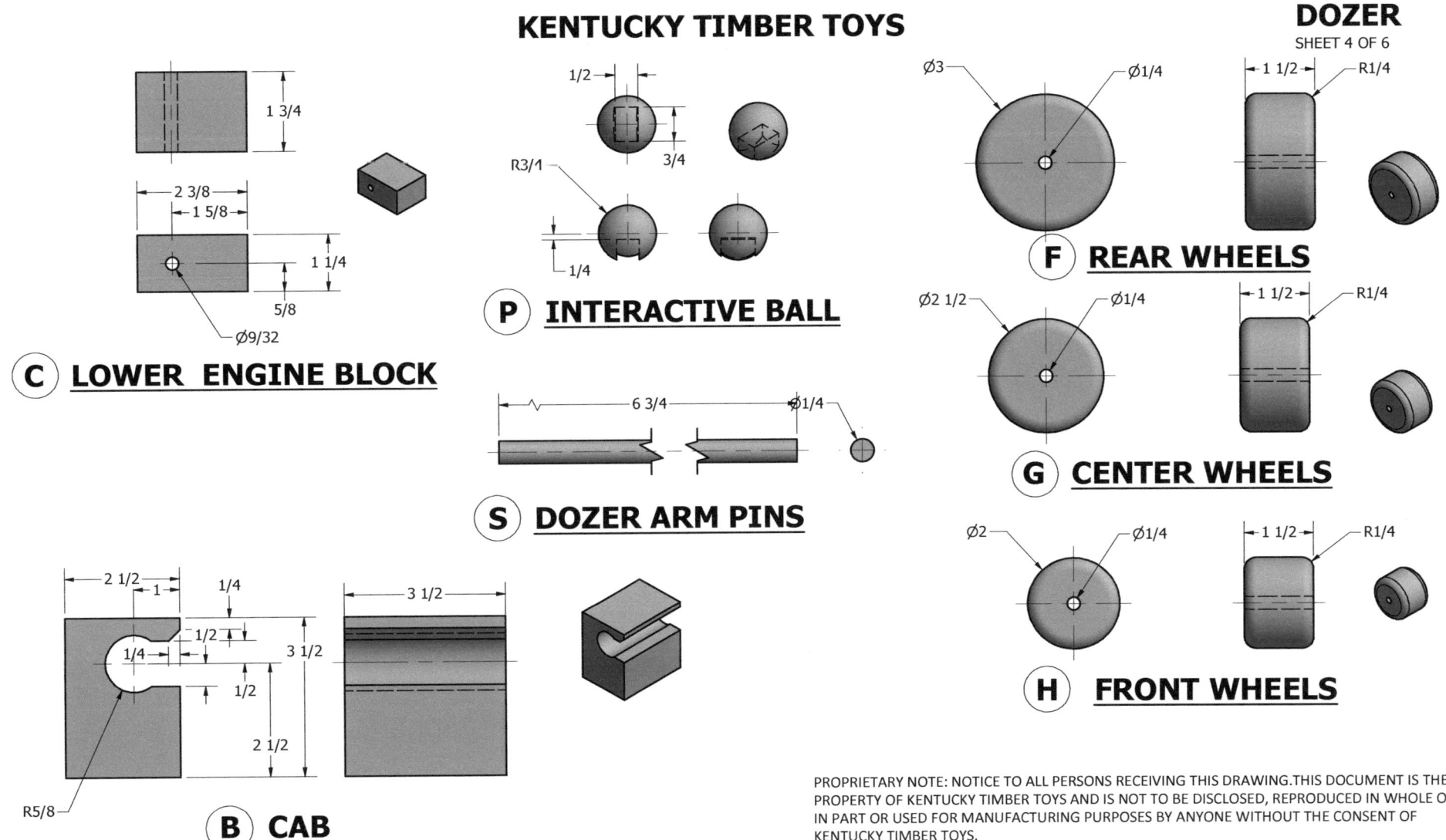

1 3/4

2 3/8
1 5/8
1 1/4
5/8
Ø9/32

C LOWER ENGINE BLOCK

1/2
3/4
R3/1
1/4

P INTERACTIVE BALL

6 3/4
Ø1/4

S DOZER ARM PINS

2 1/2
1
1/4
1/2
1/4
1/2
3 1/2
1/2
2 1/2
R5/8
3 1/2

B CAB

Ø3
Ø1/4
1 1/2
R1/4

F REAR WHEELS

Ø2 1/2
Ø1/4
1 1/2
R1/4

G CENTER WHEELS

Ø2
Ø1/4
1 1/2
R1/4

H FRONT WHEELS

Make sure you read, understand and follow all of the safety instructions that come with your power tools.

KENTUCKY TIMBER TOYS

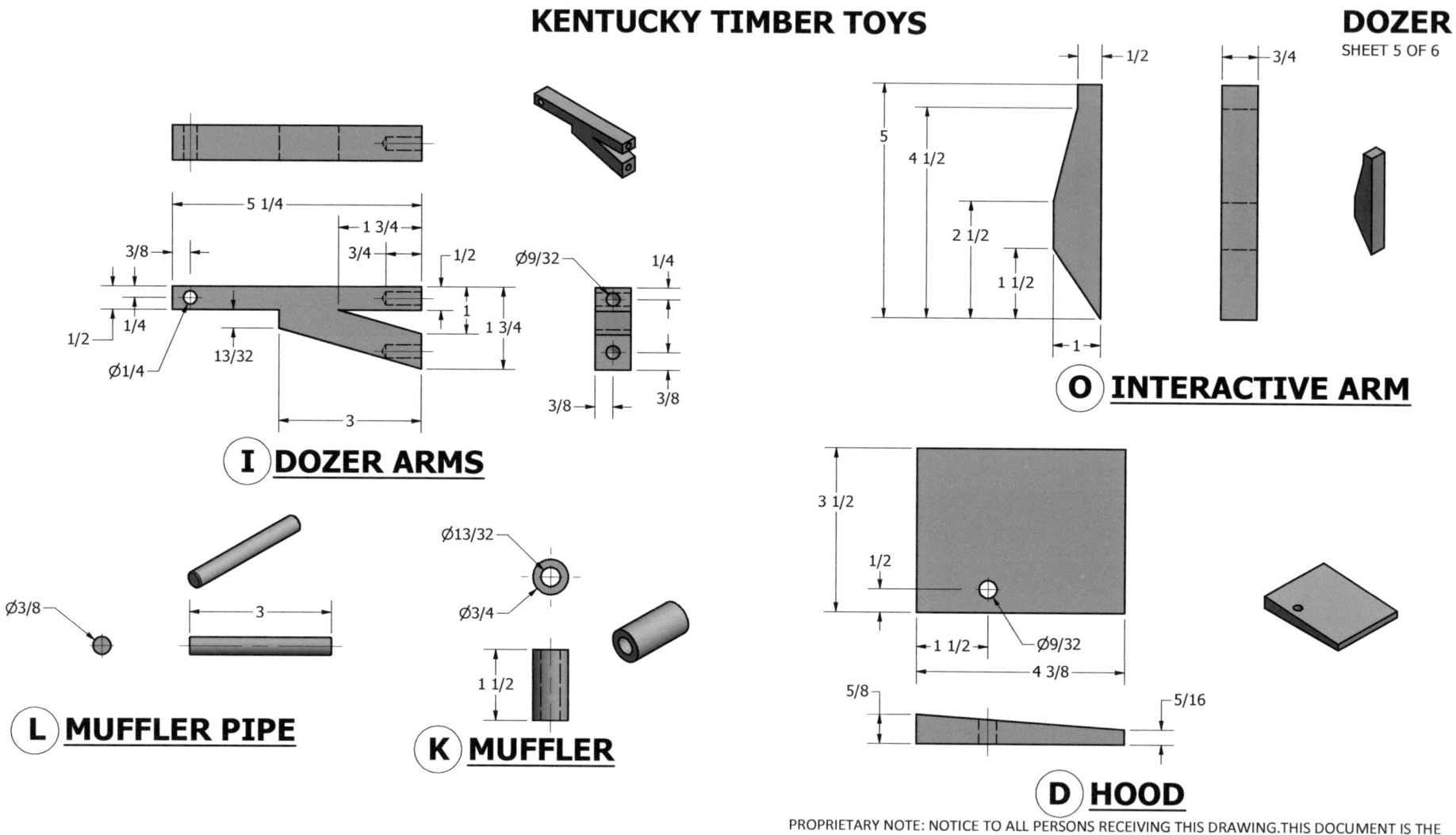

I DOZER ARMS

O INTERACTIVE ARM

L MUFFLER PIPE

K MUFFLER

D HOOD

Make sure you read, understand and follow all of the safety instructions that come with your power tools.

KENTUCKY TIMBER TOYS

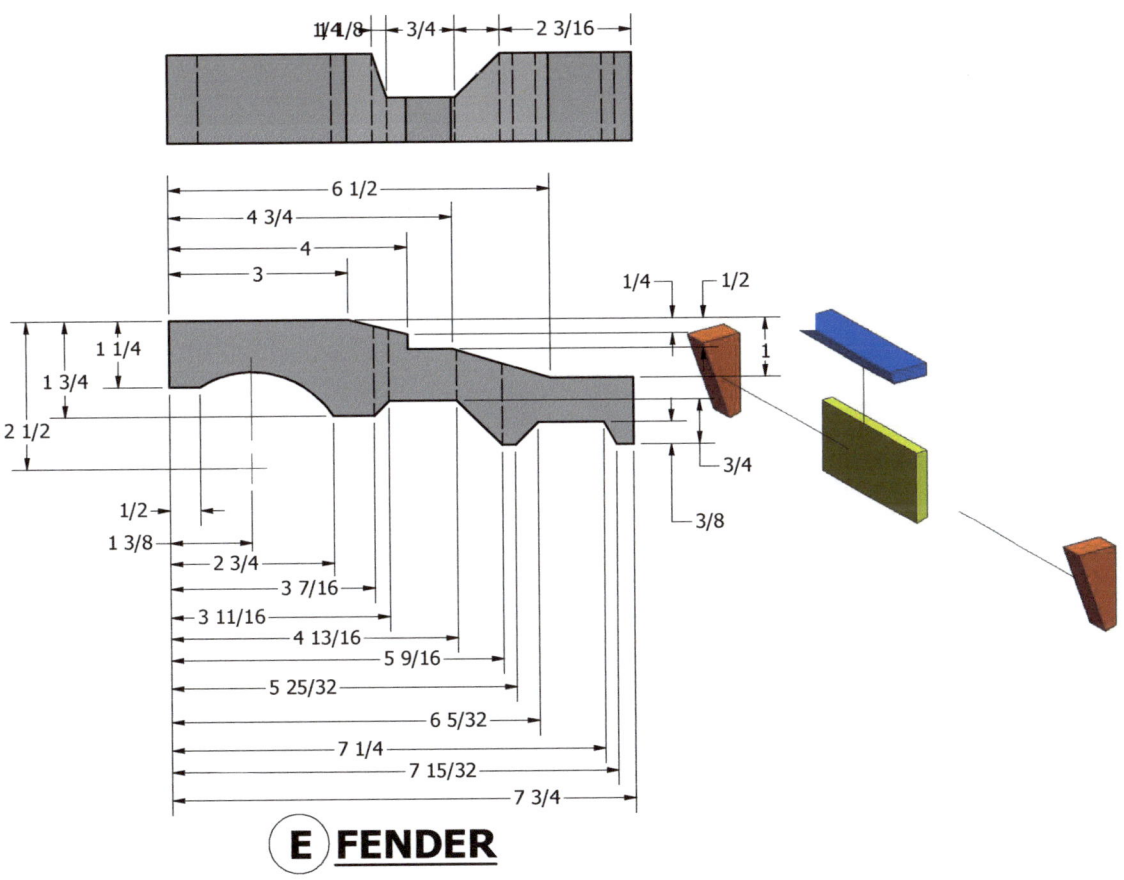

DOZER

SHEET 6 OF 6

E FENDER

Make sure you read, understand and follow all of the safety instructions that come with your power tools.

THE KENTUCKY TIMBER FRONT END LOADER

The Front-End Loader that you are about to build is one of the most versatile toys we have and is coveted by the children. We made ours 18 inches long, 6 ½ inches wide and 7 ½ inches tall. It also works with all the toys in the Construction set that we have developed.

Tools Recommended:

Drill / Drill Press	Sander / Drum Sander/ Sand paper	Gorilla Wood Glue
Hammer / Mallet	¼, 9/32 and ½ Drill bits	1 and 1 ¼ Día Hole Saw
Jig Saw / Band saw	(4) – 12" Clamps	¼" round over bit
Router		

Materials Needed:

A piece of Douglas Fir 3 ½ x 3 ½ x 12 ½ (This will make parts A, B, C and I)

A piece of 2 x 4 x 10 white Pine (this will make parts D, E and F)

¼ Dowel Rod (comes in 48" lengths), this will make part N)

½ Dowel Rod (comes in 48" lengths), this will make part H)

1 x 4 x 36 white / yellow pine or poplar (this will make parts G, J, K, L and P)

2 x 6 x 24 white / yellow pine (this will make all 4 parts of part M)

1 ¼ Día Wooden Ball (This can be purchased at any hobby shop. Makes part O)

Make sure you read, understand and follow all of the safety instructions that come with your power tools.

Layout:

The Cab (part A), The Front end (part B) and the Rear End (part C) are all cut from the Douglas Fir in the material listing. We chose Douglas Fir for the color contrast, ease of shaping and sanding, cost containment and the finished appearance. When you get to cutting and drilling the parts it will be easier and safer to drill all your holes, as indicated in drawings, prior to cutting them out. The larger block provides better stability and better clamping or hand hold surface area than the small cut out pieces.

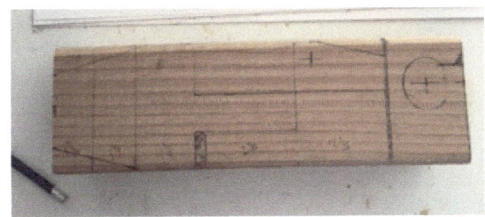 

Drill the 1 ¼ inch hole into the Cab (Part A), the Hole saw will not go all the way through. We used the band saw to cut the remaining wood out. You can use a 1 ¼ Forstner bit to drill the circle out and then a band saw or copping saw to finish the cuts. Once done, cut the cab off of the large piece. Don't worry about the hole in the bottom of the cab at this time. You will drill that later in the assembly. Now, your cab is 2 ¾ inches wide (not the full 3 ½") that the wood is. Looking at the drawings, you will see that the top view shows a ¾ inch piece removed from the cab. Do not forget to complete this step. Cut it off from the larger piece and set aside

 You can use an oscillating sander or a drum sander in a drill press, to get the inside of the cab smooth and a 1 x 30 belt sander to complete the rest. Later you will router or sand all the side of the cab to remove all the sharp edges.

The next step is to cut the vertical lines of the main body front end and rear end pieces. Then a ¼ inch slot needs to be kerf cut so that your saw blade will fit in sideways for the separation cut.

Once the verticle cuts are made you can now slip the blade in sideways and cut the remaining parts out as shown and you should end up with what is in picture below.

Once all the main body pieces are cut out move onto the individual parts. Part B (the Front End) and C (The Rear End) drill a 9/32 hole in the front end of part B all the way through the part. This will hold the front bucket in place later in the build. Now cut the ¾ pieces off both sides of the front end.

Make sure you read, understand and follow all of the safety instructions that come with your power tools.

Draw out the articulating curve and mark the counter bore and straight hole as indicated for the front end. Then shape the rear end (part C) with the angles indicated on the diagram and draw out the articulation curve as shown on the drawing. (Shown below)

 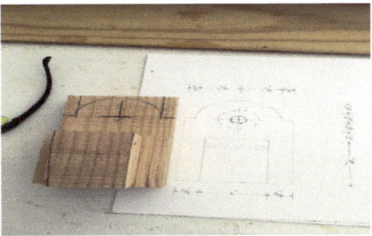

Now, shape the rear end (part C) with the angles indicated on the diagram and draw out the articulation curve as shown on the drawing. (Shown below)

Tape the pieces together and drill the counter bore (1 ¼ diameter and 5/8 inch deep). The forstner bit will provide you a center punch in the counter bore. Drill a ½ inch hole all the way through both pieces. This will make sure that your holes are aligned for proper assembly later. Now cut out the articulation circle on both pieces.

 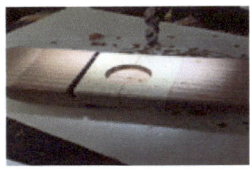 

At this point parts A, B and C should be completely cut out and routered to take all the sharp edges off the parts and sanded to your preference.

Make sure you read, understand and follow all of the safety instructions that come with your power tools.   41

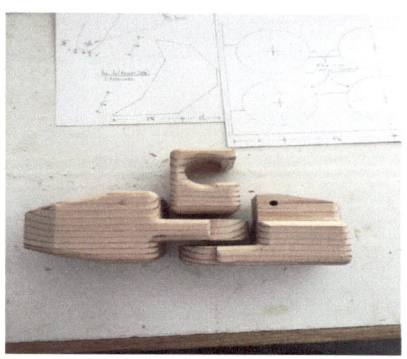

Start phase 2, the wheels (Part F) and fenders (Parts D and E). You will be making these out of a 2 x 6. You will get both front and rear fenders and all four tires from 17-inch-long piece. Once you cut them out with the 3-inch hole saw and the band saw, sand and router all the pieces to remove all the sharp edges.

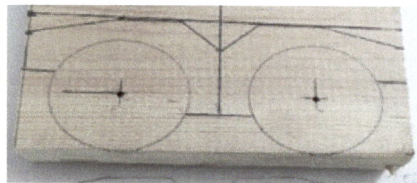

Now cut out the wheel hubs (Parts P) and drill a 9/32 hole through them and cut the Axles from the ¼ dowel rod. Sand and router to your preference. Assemble of what you have completed so far. Build the pivot pin and retention cap (Parts G and R). Center and glue the cab (part A) to the rear end (Part C) on the articulation circle and clamp in place. Once it is dry you will use the ½ hole in Rear End (Part C) as a guide to drill the ½ hole into the cab 1" deep. With that completed now slip the Pivot pin and retaining cap (parts G and R) through the front end (part B) and glue it into the cab (parts A). Make sure tha the two pieces pivot freely.

Make sure you read, understand and follow all of the safety instructions that come with your power tools.

Take the wheels (Part F) and place an axle (Part Q) into one of them. It will be a press fit, so lightly tap them into the hole that the hole saw placed into the center of them. Slide the wheel hub onto the axel and the tap the second wheel into place. This will give you wheels, axle and wheel hub as a single piece. Then glue them into place.

Once dry, glue the fenders into place leaving a ¼ gap between the wheels and the inside of the fender. You have now completed the body assembly of the front-end loader.

Start phase 3 of the build which is the bucket by using the diagram (Part M). Take a 2 x 6 and draw out 4 pieces and then cut them out. (Band saw or Jig saw) tip: we used a band saw for the ease and safety factor. Sand them as flat as possible and glue them together. Cut out the bucket sides (Parts K) and sand to match.

Once the bucket is dried you will need to sand the inside of the bucket to get a nice curve. We used a belt sander to accomplish this (pictured below). However, you can use a drum sander in a drill press or an oscillating sander (this is your personal choice and what you are comfortable with). This is going to create a great deal of dust. We recommend you hook your sander up to a shop vac or vacuum system and use a mask.

Make sure you read, understand and follow all of the safety instructions that come with your power tools.

Caps (parts K) into place and let dry.

Now that it is dry, sand the outside of the bucket to match the bucket sides. This will provide you a consistent visual appealing product and supply a nice flat section to attach the loader box and articulation arm and ball to.

Make the articulation arm (Part L) and then round over a ½ "end so that when you drill the ½ inch hole in the Ball is will fit tightly together. Glue and set aside.

While that is drying, glue and center the loader box (part I) to the bucket and let dry. Then glue and center the articulation arm and ball to the loader box and let dry.

Make sure you read, understand and follow all of the safety instructions that come with your power tools.

Finally slide the bucket pins (parts N) into the bucket arms (Parts J) and loader box (part I) and attach to the body. Glue only the outer portions of the pins to the arms. The bucket should move freely. Congratulations, you have completed the build.

PARTS LIST			
PART	QTY	DESCRIPTION	DIMENSIONS
A	1	Cab	$3\frac{1}{2} \times 2\frac{3}{4} \times 2\frac{1}{4}$
B	1	Front End	$3\frac{1}{2} \times 3\frac{1}{2} \times 5\frac{1}{2}$
C	1	Rear End	$3\frac{1}{2} \times 3\frac{1}{2} \times 7\frac{1}{4}$
D	2	Front Fenders	$1\frac{1}{2} \times 1\frac{1}{2} \times 4\frac{1}{8}$
E	2	Rear Fenders	$2\frac{1}{2} \times 1\frac{1}{2} \times 4\frac{1}{8}$
F	4	Wheels	3" DIA x $1\frac{1}{2}$
G	1	Pivot Stop	1" DIA x $\frac{3}{4}$
H	1	Dozer Pin	$\frac{1}{2}$" DIA x 3
I	1	Loader Box	$1\frac{1}{2} \times 1\frac{3}{4} \times 2$
J	2	Bucket Arms	$\frac{3}{4} \times 1\frac{3}{4} \times 6\frac{1}{2}$
K	2	Bucket Sides	$\frac{1}{2} \times 4\frac{1}{4} \times 6$
L	1	Interactive Arm	$\frac{1}{2} \times 1\frac{1}{4} \times 6$
M	4	Bucket	$1\frac{1}{2} \times 4\frac{1}{2} \times 5\frac{1}{2}$
N	2	Bucket Pins	$\frac{1}{4}$" DIA x 3
O	1	Interactive Ball	$1\frac{1}{4}$" DIA Wooden Bal
P	2	Wheel Hubs	$\frac{3}{4} \times \frac{3}{4} \times 3\frac{1}{2}$
Q	2	Axles	$\frac{1}{4}$" DIA x 6
R	1	Pivot Pin	$\frac{1}{2}$" DIA x $2\frac{1}{2}$

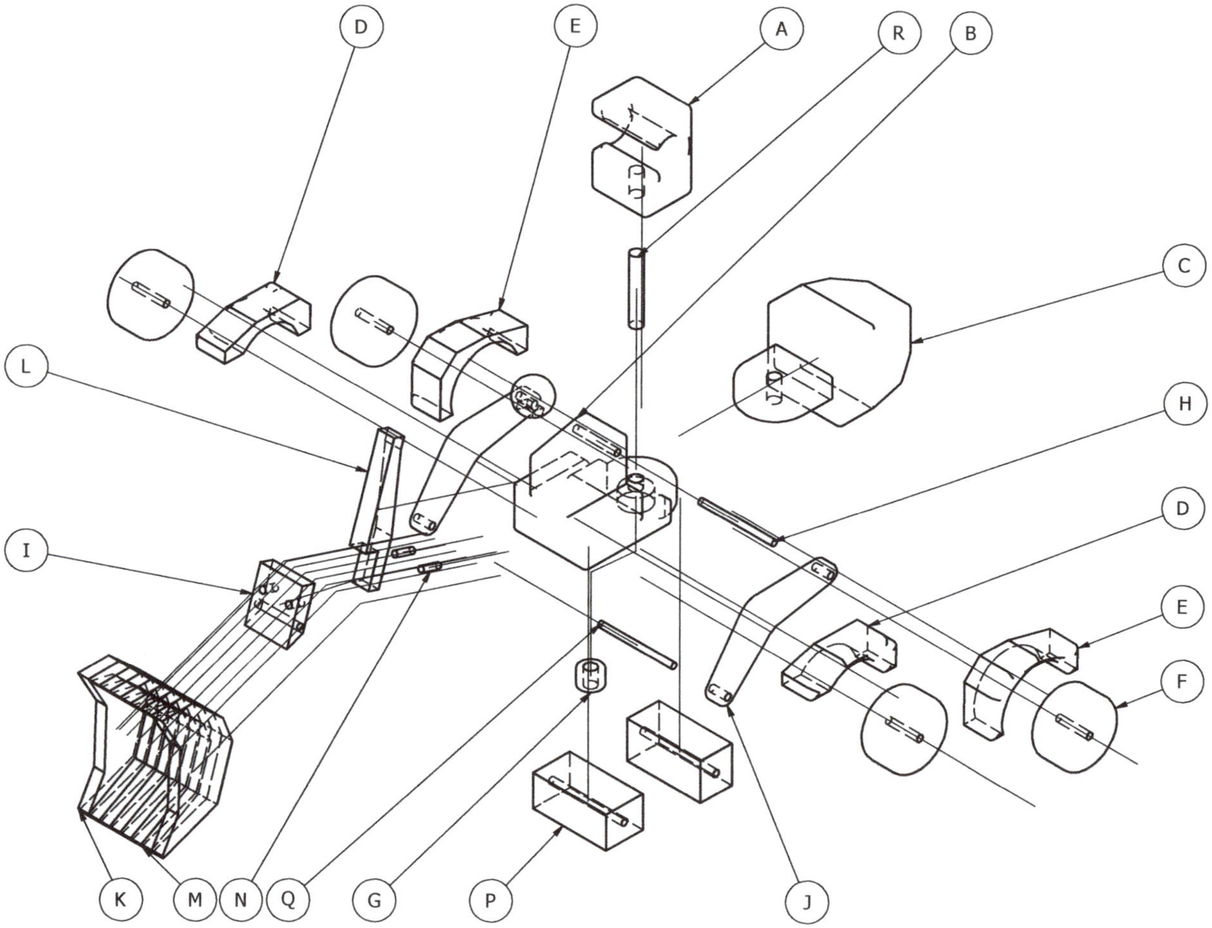

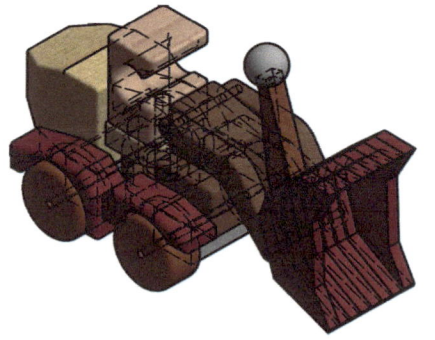

Make sure you read, understand and follow all of the safety instructions that come with your power tools.

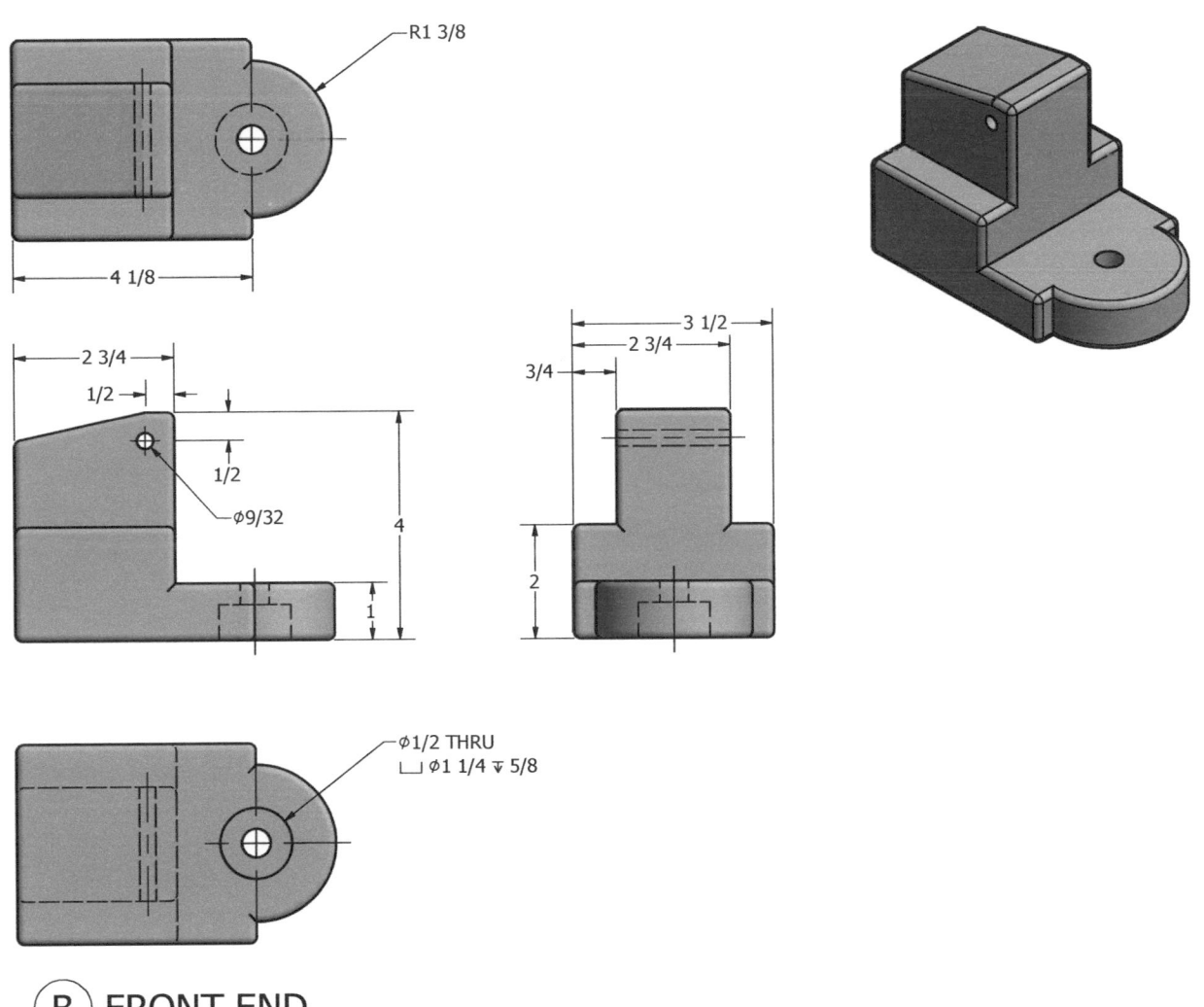

R1 3/8

4 1/8

2 3/4

1/2

1/2

ⵁ9/32

4

1

3 1/2

2 3/4

3/4

2

ⵁ1/2 THRU
⌴ ⵁ1 1/4 ▼ 5/8

(B) FRONT END

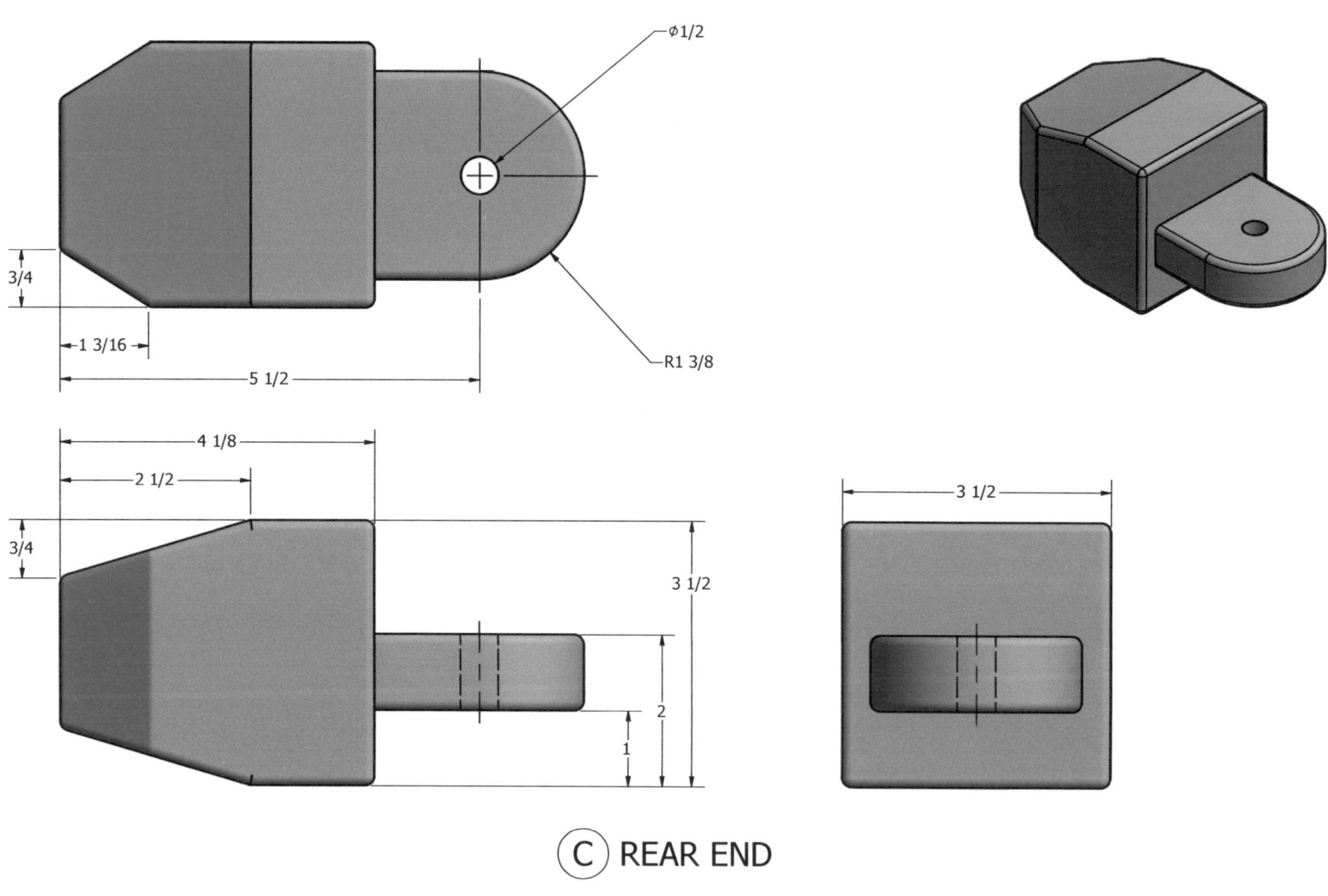

ø1/2

3/4

1 3/16

5 1/2

R1 3/8

4 1/8

2 1/2

3/4

3 1/2

3 1/2

2

1

(C) REAR END

Make sure you read, understand and follow all of the safety instructions that come with your power tools.

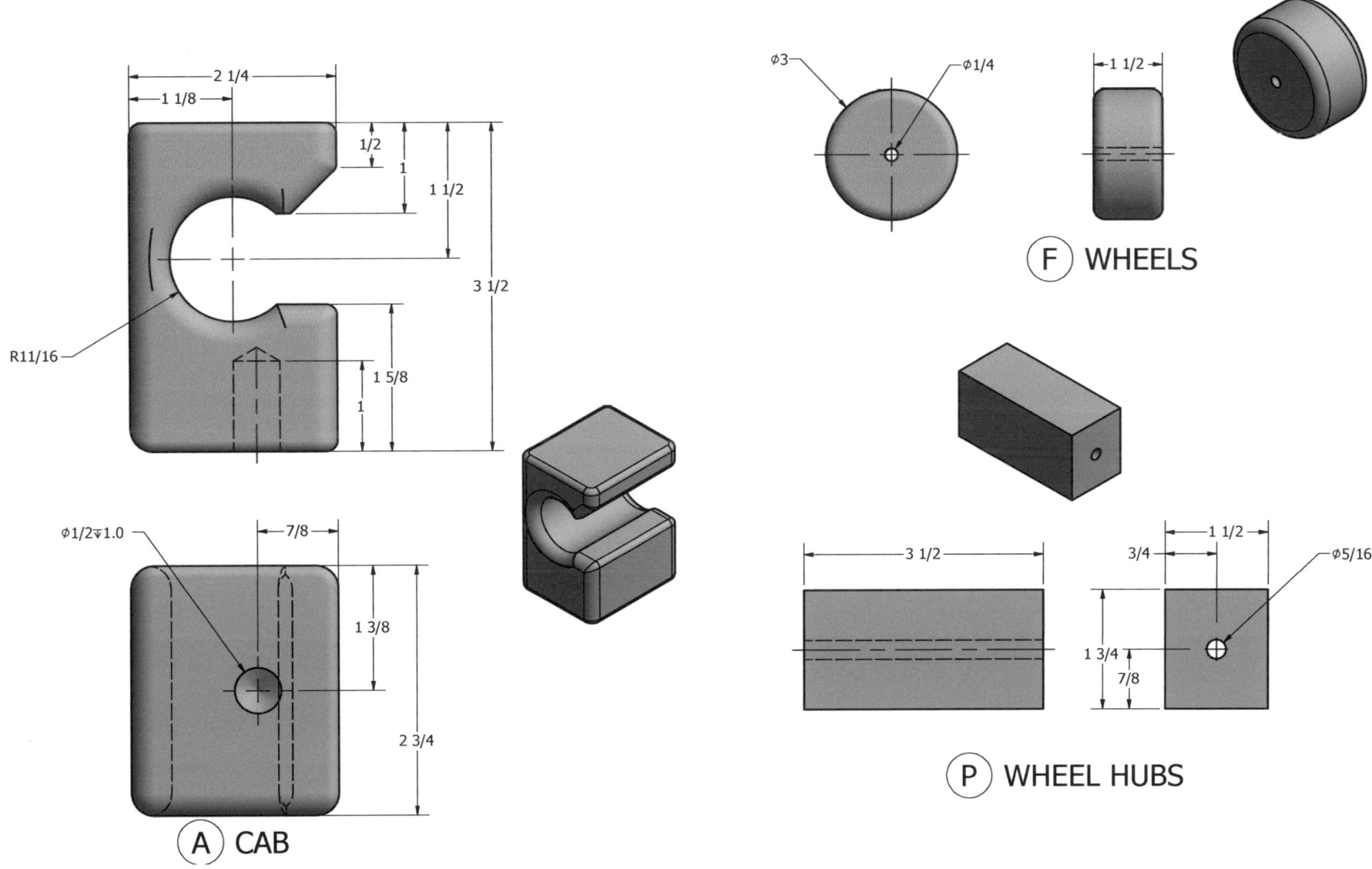

2 1/4
1 1/8
1/2
1
1 1/2
3 1/2
R11/16
1 5/8
1

ø3
ø1/4
1 1/2

(F) WHEELS

ø1/2⌶1.0
7/8
1 3/8
2 3/4

(A) CAB

3 1/2
1 1/2
3/4
1 3/4
7/8
ø5/16

(P) WHEEL HUBS

Make sure you read, understand and follow all of the safety instructions that come with your power tools.

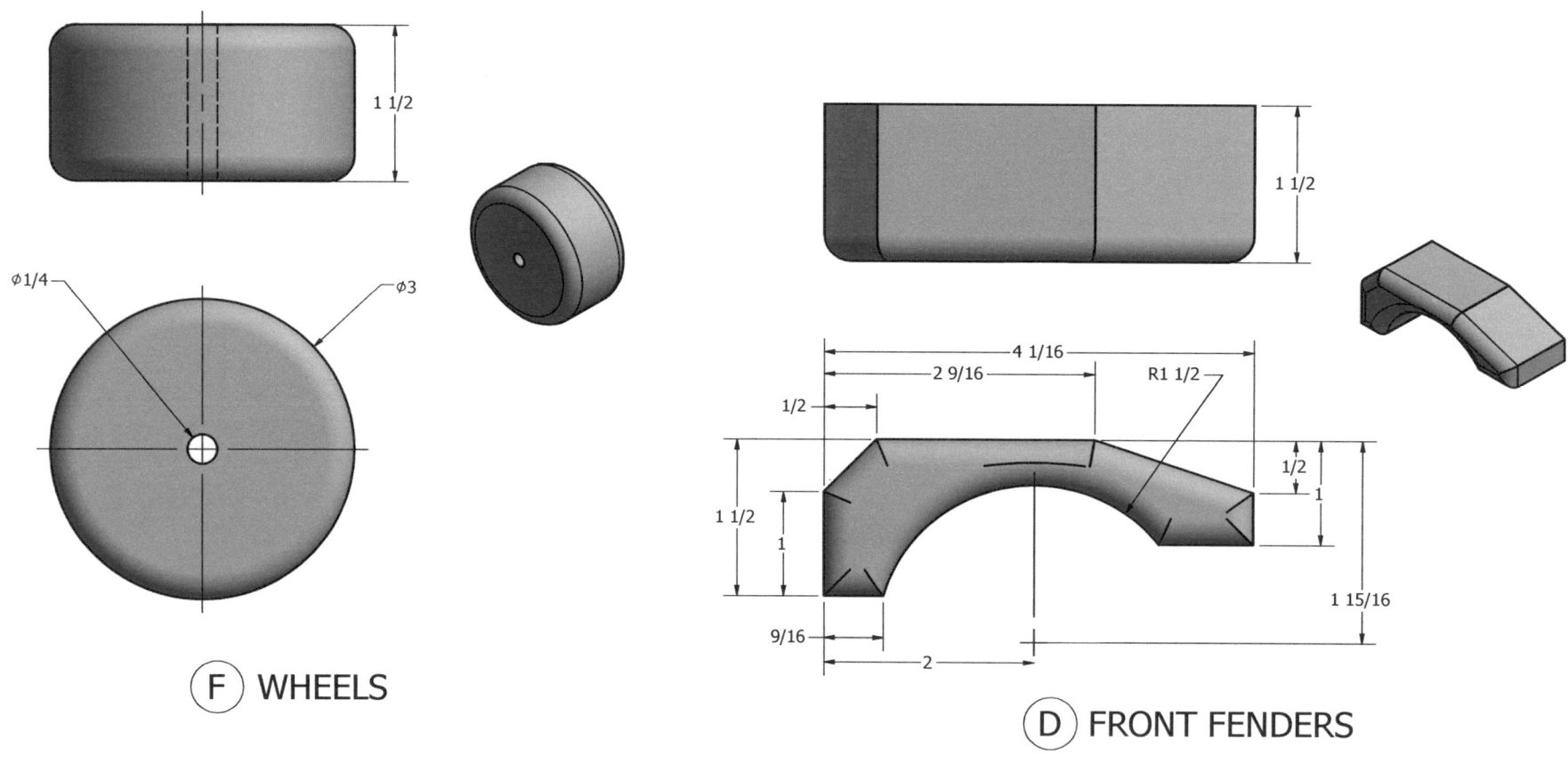

F WHEELS

D FRONT FENDERS

Make sure you read, understand and follow all of the safety instructions that come with your power tools.

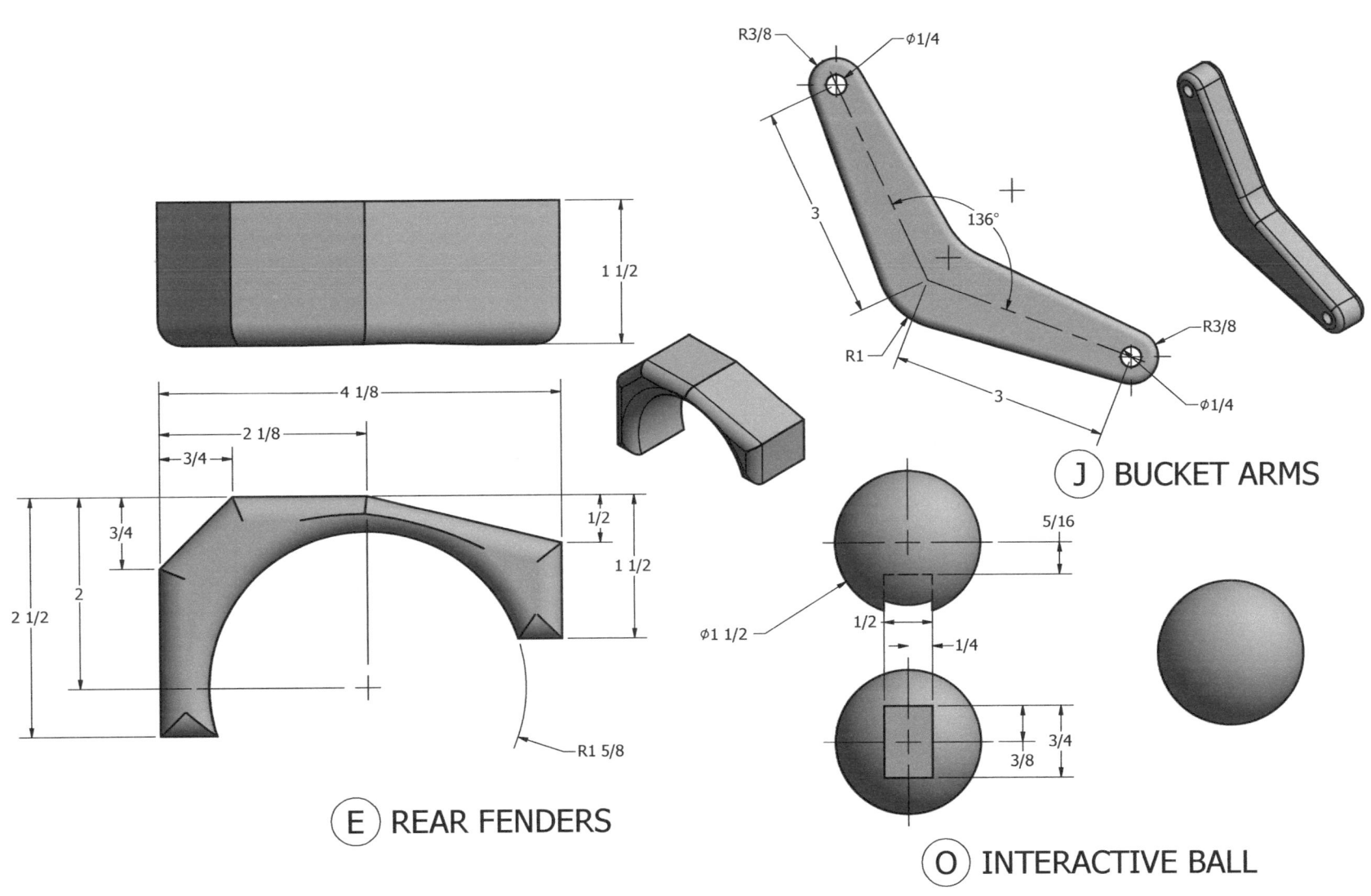

1 1/2

R3/8
φ1/4
3
136°
3
R1
R3/8
φ1/4

(J) BUCKET ARMS

4 1/8
2 1/8
3/4
3/4
1/2
1 1/2
2
2 1/2
R1 5/8

(E) REAR FENDERS

5/16
φ1 1/2
1/2
1/4
3/4
3/8

(O) INTERACTIVE BALL

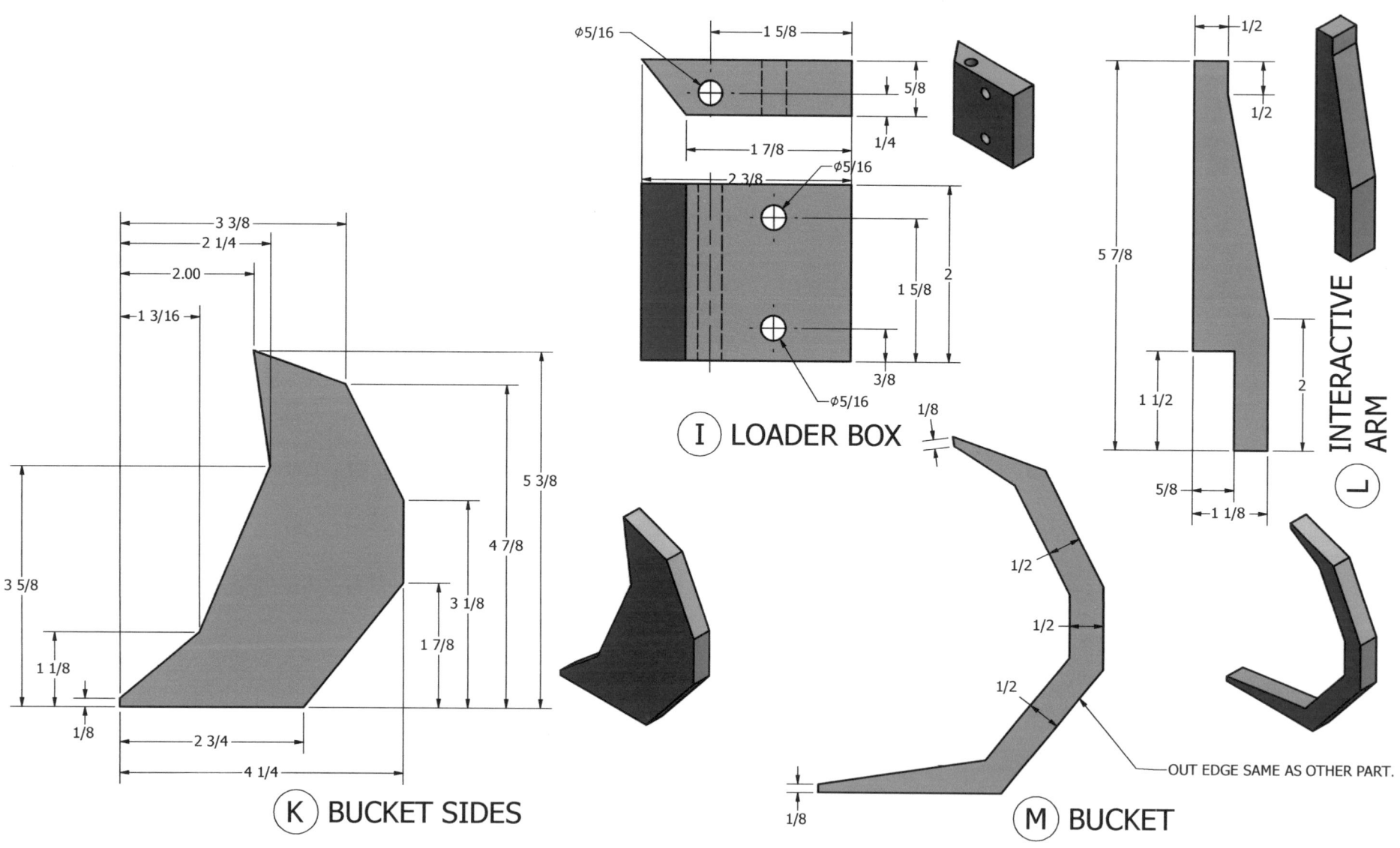

φ5/16
1 5/8
5/8
1/4
1 7/8
2 3/8
φ5/16
2
1 5/8
3/8
φ5/16

Ⓘ LOADER BOX

1/2
1/2

5 7/8

1 1/2

5/8
1 1/8

2

Ⓛ INTERACTIVE ARM

3 3/8
2 1/4
2.00
1 3/16

5 3/8
4 7/8
3 1/8
1 7/8

3 5/8

1 1/8

1/8

2 3/4
4 1/4

Ⓚ BUCKET SIDES

1/8

1/2

1/2

1/2

OUT EDGE SAME AS OTHER PART.

1/8
1/8

Ⓜ BUCKET

Make sure you read, understand and follow all of the safety instructions that come with your power tools.

THE KENTUCKY TIMBER EXCAVATOR

This is one of the more challenging toys to build and does take some time and equipment to complete it. There are a total of 23 parts and 39 pieces that will have to be cut out and sanded prior to assembly.

Recommended Tools Needed:

Drill press	1" belt Sander	White Wood Glue	Hammer / Mallet	1 ½ Dia Forstner Bit
1/8, 9/32, ½ and 1/4 Drill bits	1 ¼ Dia Hole Saw	Band saw / scroll saw	2 – 6" Bar Clamps	
4- 2" spring clamps	¼ "round over bit and router	flush trim saw	3" and 1 ¼ Dia Hole Saw	

Materials Needed:

A piece of ½ x 6 x 36 popular

A piece of Popular ¼ x 6 x 3 ft

A piece of Yellow Pine that is 1 ½ " x 5 ½" x 24" (we used a piece of 2 x 6 x 24)

A piece of Douglas Fir that is 3 ½ x 3 ½ x 9 (basic 4 x 4 x 9)

A 1 ½ inch diameter wooden ball (you can pick this up at any craft shop)

A piece of 1/8 dowel rod (comes in 36" length)

A piece of ¼ dowel rod (comes in 36" length)

A piece of ½ dowel rod (comes in 36" length)

A bottle of wood glue (we use Tite Bond II exterior wood glue)

Layout:

The first layout will be of the Cab (Part F), turn table (Part G) and engine plate (Part S). This is made out of a single piece of 4 x 4 x 9 ½ inch Douglas Fir. We chose this for the color contrast, ease of shaping and sanding, cost containment and the finished appearance. When you get to the cutting and drilling phase it will be easier and safer to drill al your holes as indicated in the raw material prior to cutting them out. The larger block provides better stability and better clamping or hand hold surface then the small cut out pieces.

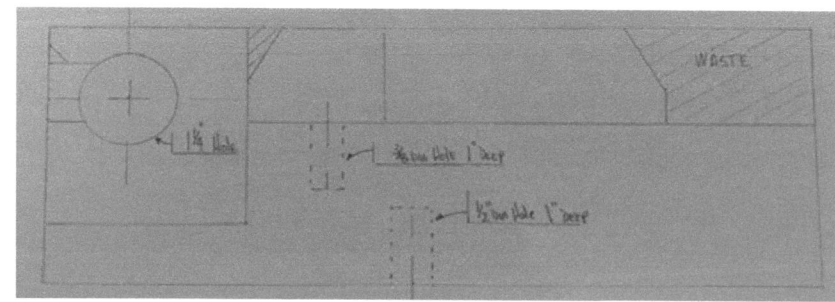

Make sure you read, understand and follow all of the safety instructions that come with your power tools.

Next layout and cut the Body (Part A) which is another piece of 4 x 4 x 9 ½ Douglas Fir. Mark your holes for the wheels in wood prior to cutting it to shape. Then lay out the fenders (Part C), the bucket (Part B) and the wheels (Parts D and E) on a piece of 2 x 4 x 48 inches pine. Finally, the excavator boom assembly (Parts K, L and M) on a piece of ½ inch x 6-inch x 36-inch poplar board. The remainder of your parts will be cut from the material left over. Finish cutting all the remaining parts out and sand the edges smooth.

Cutting and Drilling:

Using a band saw and a drill press for ease and precision, take the 4 x 4 x 48 Douglas Fir and drill out all your holes as indicated on the plans. Then cut out the parts A (the base), F (The Cab), G (The Turn Table) and S (the Engine Plate). The Wheels (parts D and E) will be the next step. Using a 3" and a 2" hole saw in the drill press, drill out the parts. Tip: you may want to drill about ¾ of the way through and then flip the board and finish drilling from the other side. This will prevent tear out and leave you with a smoother edge. Using that same piece of pine, cut out the shape for part B, the bucket interior. Now cut out the fenders (part C).

At this point you should be able to cut out the fender sections (as shown in the drawing)

Remember to fan cut the fender wells first and then follow the lines to cut the curves of the fenders. This will prevent the saw blade from pinching or worse, breaking. Finally cut out and fit the body spacer (Part H) in between the Body (part A) and the Turn table (Part G). Once you have all the parts dry you will need to drill the holes for the pivot pin and cap (parts P and Q) that holds the upper and lower assemblies together. Make your pivot pin and cap out of the ½ dowel rod and a ¾" piece of material. Glue the cap on the pivot pin and set aside to dry. Then drill a ½ hole into the upper assembly 1 ¼ inch deep centered on the bottom of the upper assembly. When dry fit the pivot pin and cap through the lower assembly and then (with glue in the hole of the upper assembly) push the pivot pin into it and let dry. The upper assembly should move freely from the lower assembly when dry.

Once you have the main body piece cut out it should look similar to the picture below when dry fitted together.

The wheel holes in the body base (part A) are drilled with a 9/32 drill bit so that the ¼ inch Axles (part R) will spin freely once the wheels are attached (parts D and E). Router the edges of all the large pieces with a ¼ inch round over bit on a router table only do the edges that you are comfortable with. Routering small pieces can be dangerous, if you are not comfortable with using a router, just sand the edges over smooth. The fenders are a mirror of each other and that the round over only happens on the side that will be facing outward.

The cutting out of the excavator arm parts is pretty straight forward. We cut them just outside of the lines and then with a small 1" belt sander brought it down to the lines as indicated in the drawings. Now that all the pieces are cut out, sanding all the rough edges and cleaning up the surfaces is the next step. This helps prevent any splintering and provides the finished product that the child will be playing with, a nice smooth surfaced edge. This can be accomplished by using a power sander or just good old fashion sandpaper and elbow grease. To start the assembly glue the excavator arm together. The spacer (part L) will need to be laminated between the excavator main boom (parts K). The excavator cab (part I) will need to be glued to the excavator cab deck (part I). Tip: Once the glue is applied secure the parts together with 2-inch spring clamps (as shown): You can do a final sanding and shaping on the boom arm assembly and get it to look how you want.

Once dry we can then glue the support arm brackets into place (part J) and evenly space them. When they are dry you will need to now drill a

Make sure you read, understand and follow all of the safety instructions that come with your power tools.

¼ inch hole through both support brackets and the excavator boom and the cab. The hole should be 1 ½ inches deep. Then insert the base pin main boom (part V). This will require a little tapping with a mallet or hammer to get it into place. Glue and clamp everything into place and set aside to dry. You will cut off any excess of the pin with the trim saw once the assembly is dry.

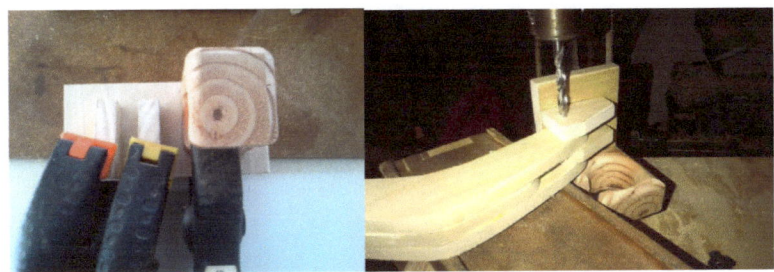

While the upper half of the excavator is drying, begin assembling the base by gluing the body spacer (part H) onto the excavator base (part A) and then set the fenders into place flush with the top of body spacer and then glued the rest onto the excavator base (part A). drill the 1 ½ hole in the bottom of the body (as indicated on the drawings) and then the ½ center hole for the pivot pin to fit into. Now that the upper assembly is dry turn the cab deck over and drill four 1/8 "holes through the cab deck into the gussets. Place some glue into the holes and drive four pieces of 1/8 "dowel rod (part W) into the holes and then cut them off flush with a trim saw. Sand as needed. Then drill a ¼" hole through the cab deck into the cab 1/2 "deep. Place some glue into the hole and drive a ¼ "dowel ½ "long into the hole and sand as needed. This step will reinforce the gussets and the cab from breaking off through use.

While that is drying the upper excavator assembly will need the interactive arm and ball glued together and then attached to the boom by drilling a ¼" hole through all three pieces and then driving a ¼ dowel through the hole while only gluing the two boom pieces to the pin. This will allow the interactive arm to move freely. Now you can glue the interactive ball onto the arm (Right picture above) and the cab deck (with Gussets and cab pinned together) to the excavator body and set aside to dry. Cutting out the scoop will start by cutting the diagrams out of part B. Then use the band saw, jig saw or copping saw to cut the shape out as provided on the diagram and glue them together to form the inside of the scoop. Once you have the glue up completed sand the scoop to its desired shape, for this step we used an isolating sander. Once dry, then glue the two side pieces (part J) into place, clamp and let dry. Final sanding of the external shape of the scoop should be done at this time.

Now that the bucket is dry and the upper body assembly is dry you can now assemble the bucket to the interactive arm. Measure out a ½ inch cut centered in the upper part of the bucket and cut out the section on the band saw. Make sure you cut on the inside of the lines to ensure a tight fit when you set the arm into place (as shown in the picture below). Now glue the assembly together.

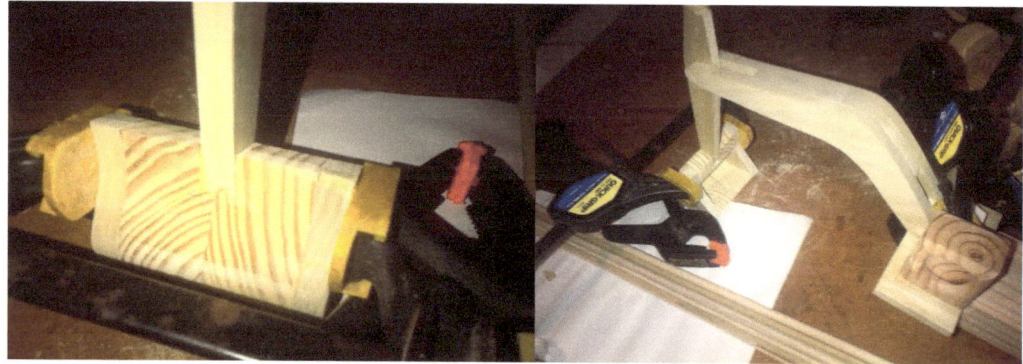

Note: If you make a mistake by making the cut out to big you can shim the space with standard door shims, glue and sand to fit, or cut the bucket in half and re-glue it together and clamp it in place.

Make sure you read, understand and follow all of the safety instructions that come with your power tools.

Now attach the cab and boom assembly to the turntable (part G) by gluing and clamping it into place. Then glue the exhaust pieces (parts T and U) into place and set aside to dry. Attach one wheel (D) to one end of the Axles (R) and then slide that assembly through the excavator base and attach the other wheel onto the Axles then glue the wheel assembly into place. Repeat this process for all the wheel assemblies. Once the glue is dried on this set of wheels your project is completed and ready for use.

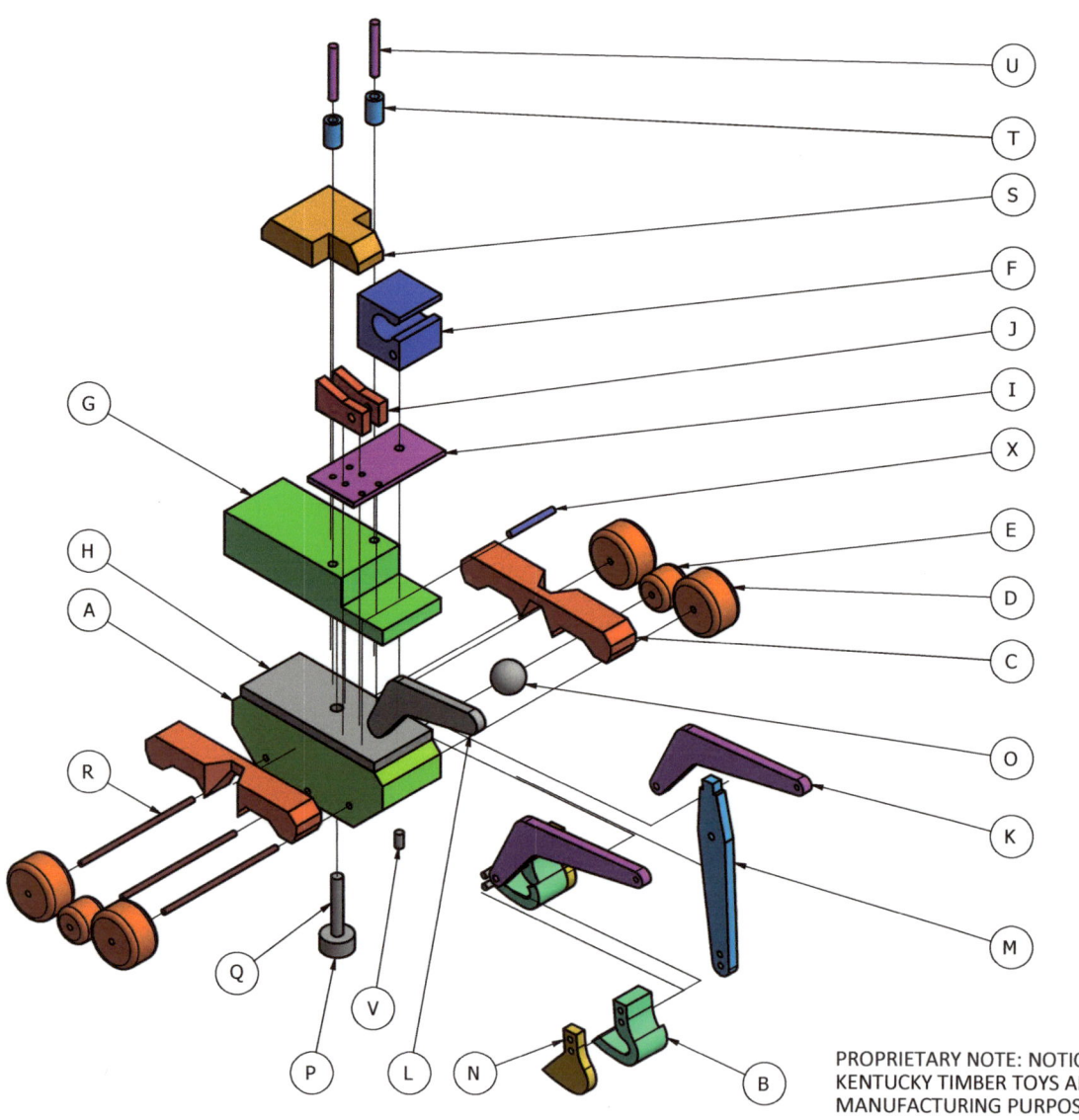

ITEM	QTY	PART NUMBER	DESCRIPTION
A	1	BODY	3 1/2 X 3 1/2 X 9
B	2	BUCKET (INTERIOR)	1 1/2 X 3 1/2 X 2
C	2	FENDERS	1 1/2 X 2 1/2 X 7 1/4
D	4	3" WHEELS	1 1/2 X 3 DIA
E	2	2" WHEELS	1 1/2 X 2 DIA
F	1	CAB	2 1/2 X 2 3/4 X 2 1/2
G	1	TURN TABLE	3 1/2 X 3 1/2 X 9 1/2
H	1	BODY SPACER	1/2 X 3 1/2 X 8
I	1	CAB DECK	1/4 X 2 3/4 X 5 1/2
J	2	ARM GUSSETS	1/2 X 2 X 1 1/4
K	2	ARM BOOMS	1/2 X 3 X 11 1/4
L	1	BOOM SPACER	1/2 X 2 X 6 1/2
M	1	INTERACTIVE ARM	1/2 X 2 X 9
N	2	BUCKET SIDES	1/2 X 3 1/2 X 2
O	1	INTERACTIVE BALL	1 1/2 DIA WOODEN BALL
P	1	PIVOT PIN	1/2 DIA X 3
Q	1	PIVOT PIN CAP	1 1/4 DIA X 3/4
R	3	AXILS	1/4 DIA X 8 1/2
S	1	ENGINE PLATE	1 1/2 X 3 1/2 X 5 1/4
T	2	EXHAUST	1 3/4 X 3/4 DIA
U	2	EXHAUST PIPE	2 3/4 X 3/8 DIA
V	1	BASE PIN	1/4 X 2 1/2
W	6	BOOM ARM GUSSET PIN	1/8 X 1
X	1	BOOM ARM PIN	3/8 X 2 1/2

KENTUCKY TIMBER TOYS

EXCAVATOR

SHEET 1 OF 8

Make sure you read, understand and follow all of the safety instructions that come with your power tools.

(PARTS LIST)

KENTUCKY TIMBER TOYS

EXCAVATOR
SHEET 2 OF 8

Make sure you read, understand and follow all of the safety instructions that come with your power tools.

KENTUCKY TIMBER TOYS

EXCAVATOR
SHEET 3 OF 8

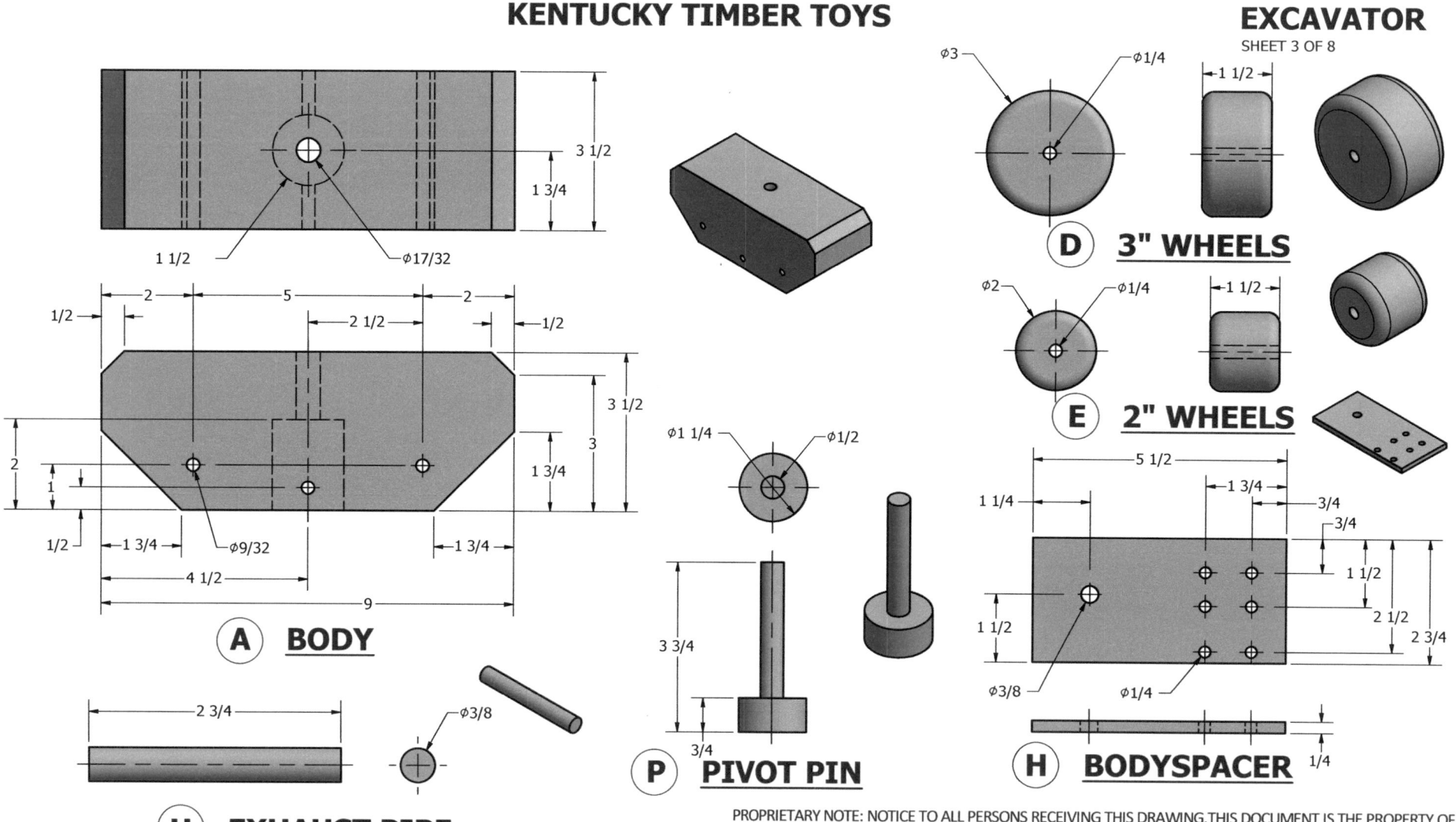

Ⓐ **BODY**

Ⓓ **3" WHEELS**

Ⓔ **2" WHEELS**

Ⓟ **PIVOT PIN**

Ⓗ **BODYSPACER**

Ⓤ **EXHAUST PIPE**

Make sure you read, understand and follow all of the safety instructions that come with your power tools.

KENTUCKY TIMBER TOYS

EXCAVATOR
SHEET 4 OF 8

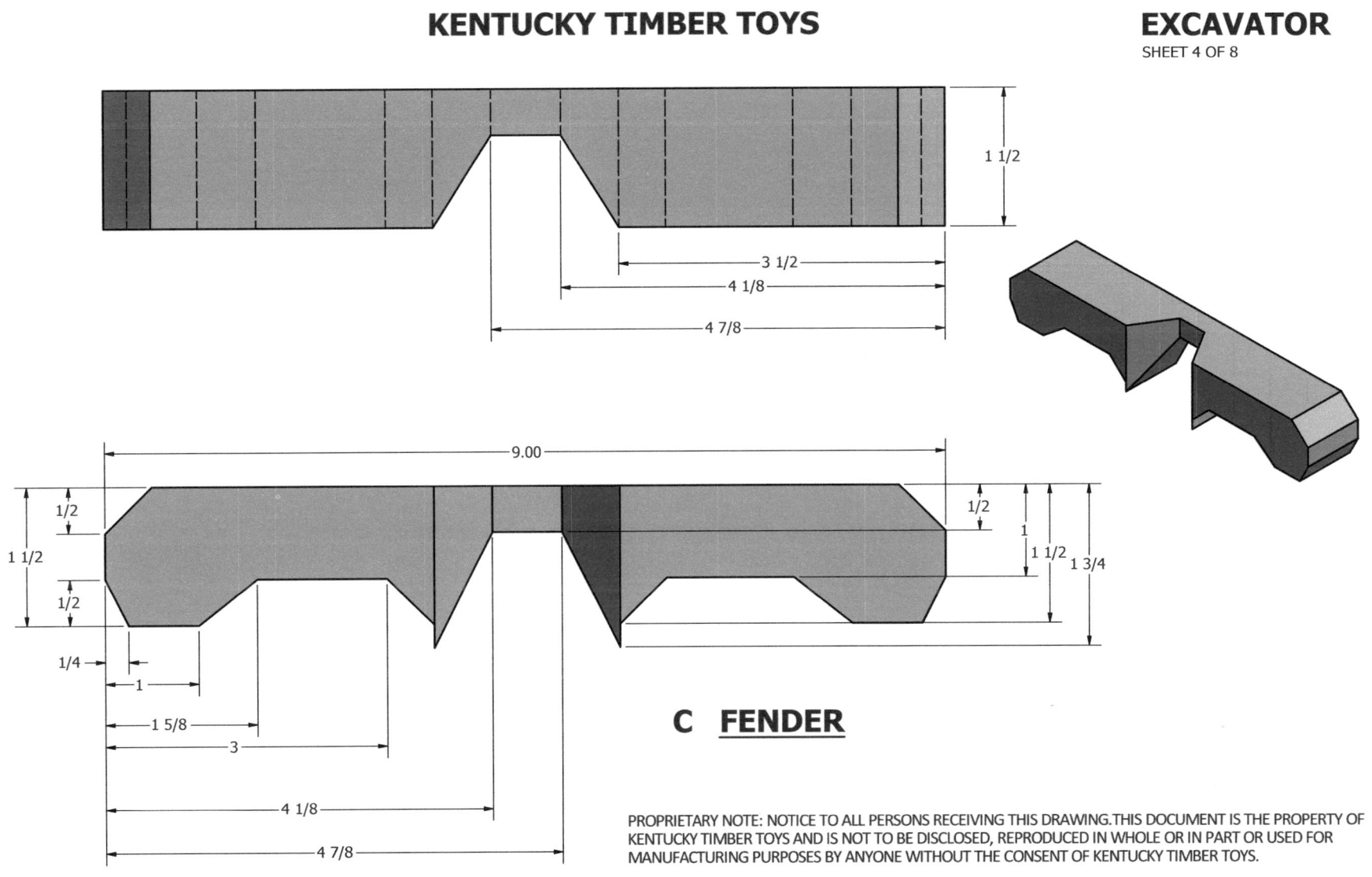

1 1/2

3 1/2

4 1/8

4 7/8

9.00

1/2

1 1/2

1/2

1/4

1

1 5/8

3

4 1/8

4 7/8

1/2

1

1 1/2   1 3/4

C   FENDER

Make sure you read, understand and follow all of the safety instructions that come with your power tools.

KENTUCKY TIMBER TOYS

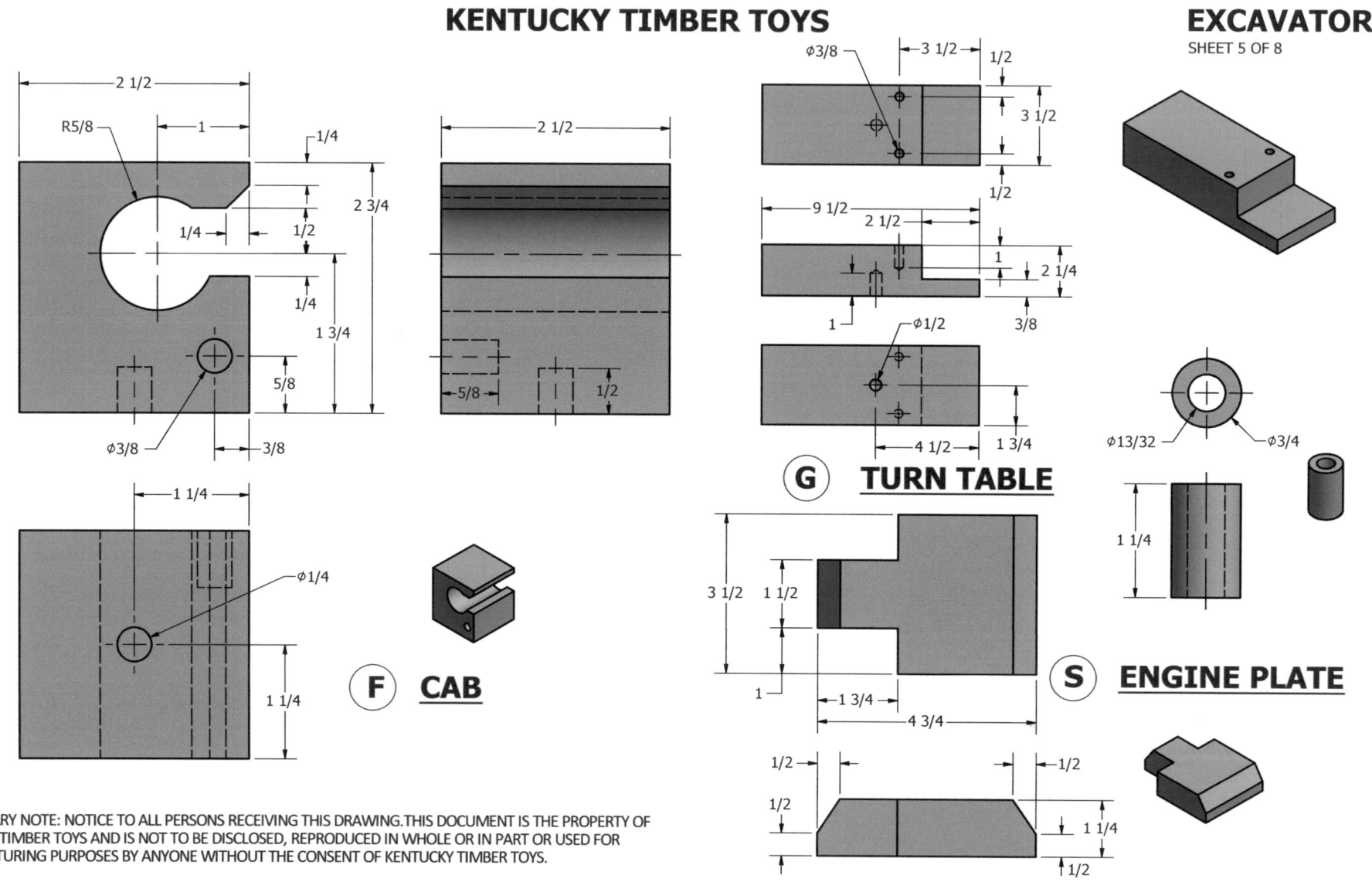

(G) **TURN TABLE**

(F) **CAB**

(S) **ENGINE PLATE**

Make sure you read, understand and follow all of the safety instructions that come with your power tools.

KENTUCKY TIMBER TOYS

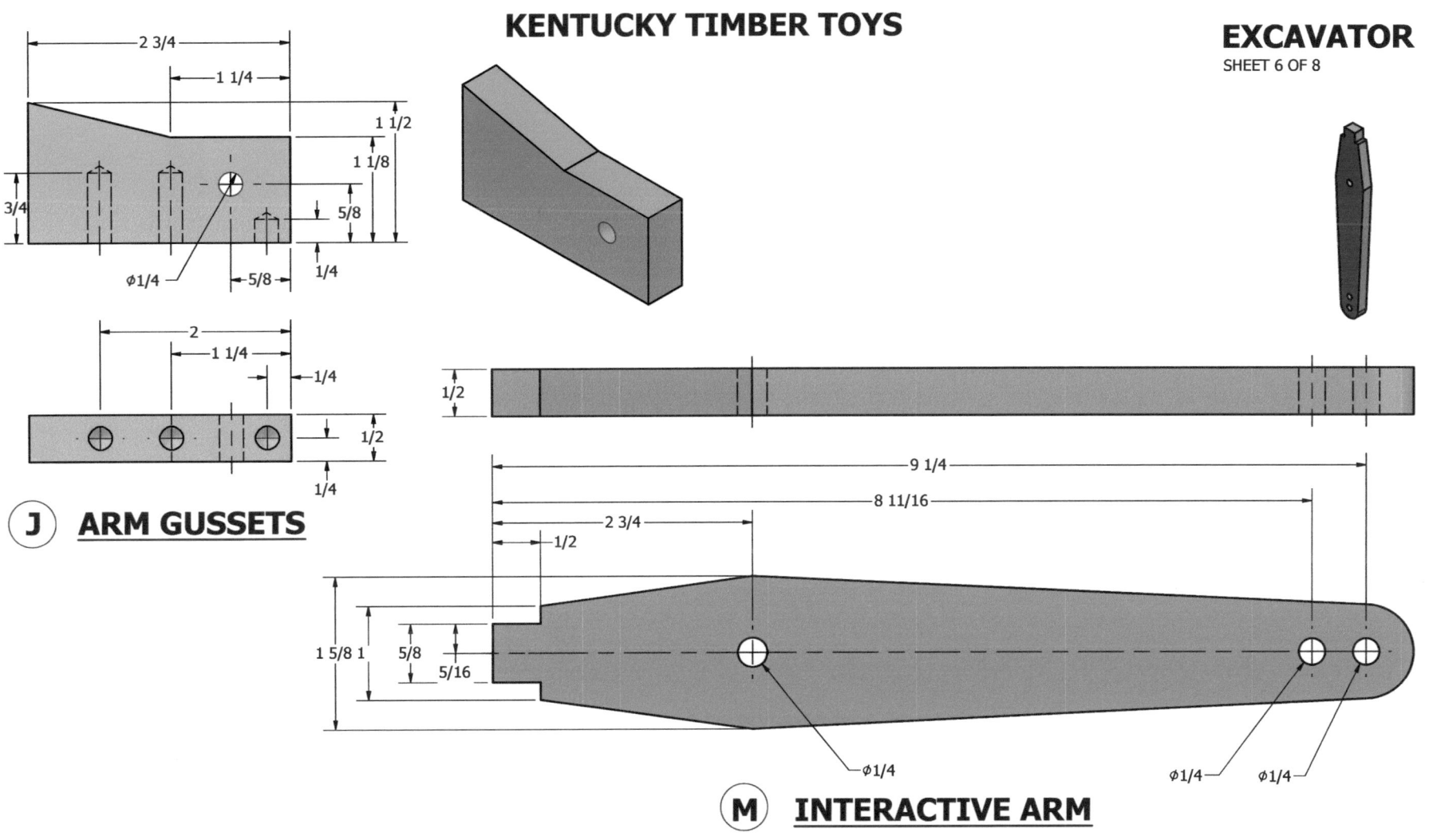

J **ARM GUSSETS**

M **INTERACTIVE ARM**

Make sure you read, understand and follow all of the safety instructions that come with your power tools.

KENTUCKY TIMBER TOYS

EXCAVATOR

SHEET 7 OF 8

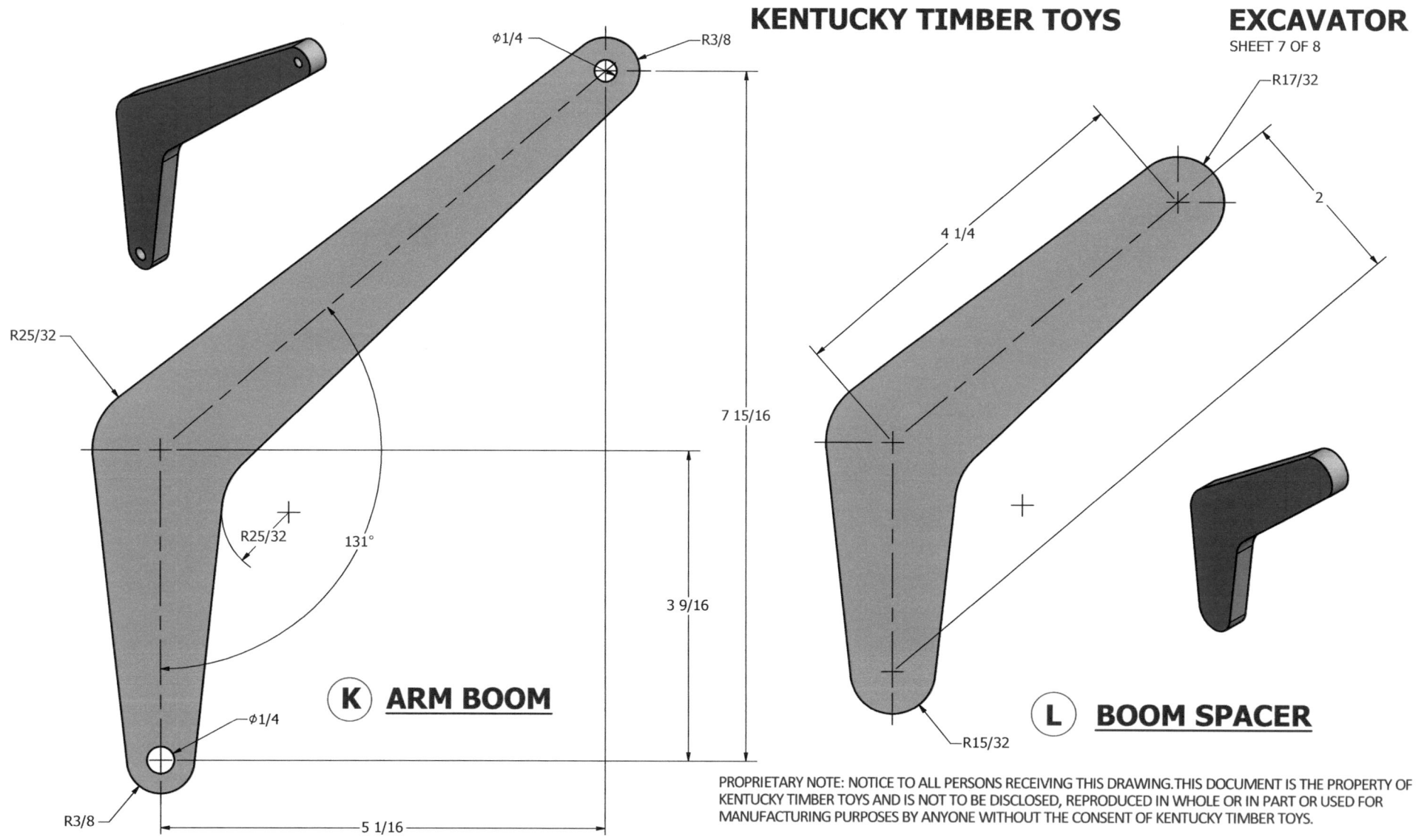

φ1/4

R3/8

R17/32

4 1/4

2

R25/32

7 15/16

R25/32

131°

3 9/16

(K) **ARM BOOM**

R15/32

(L) **BOOM SPACER**

φ1/4

R3/8

5 1/16

Make sure you read, understand and follow all of the safety instructions that come with your power tools.

KENTUCKY TIMBER TOYS

EXCAVATOR
SHEET 8 OF 8

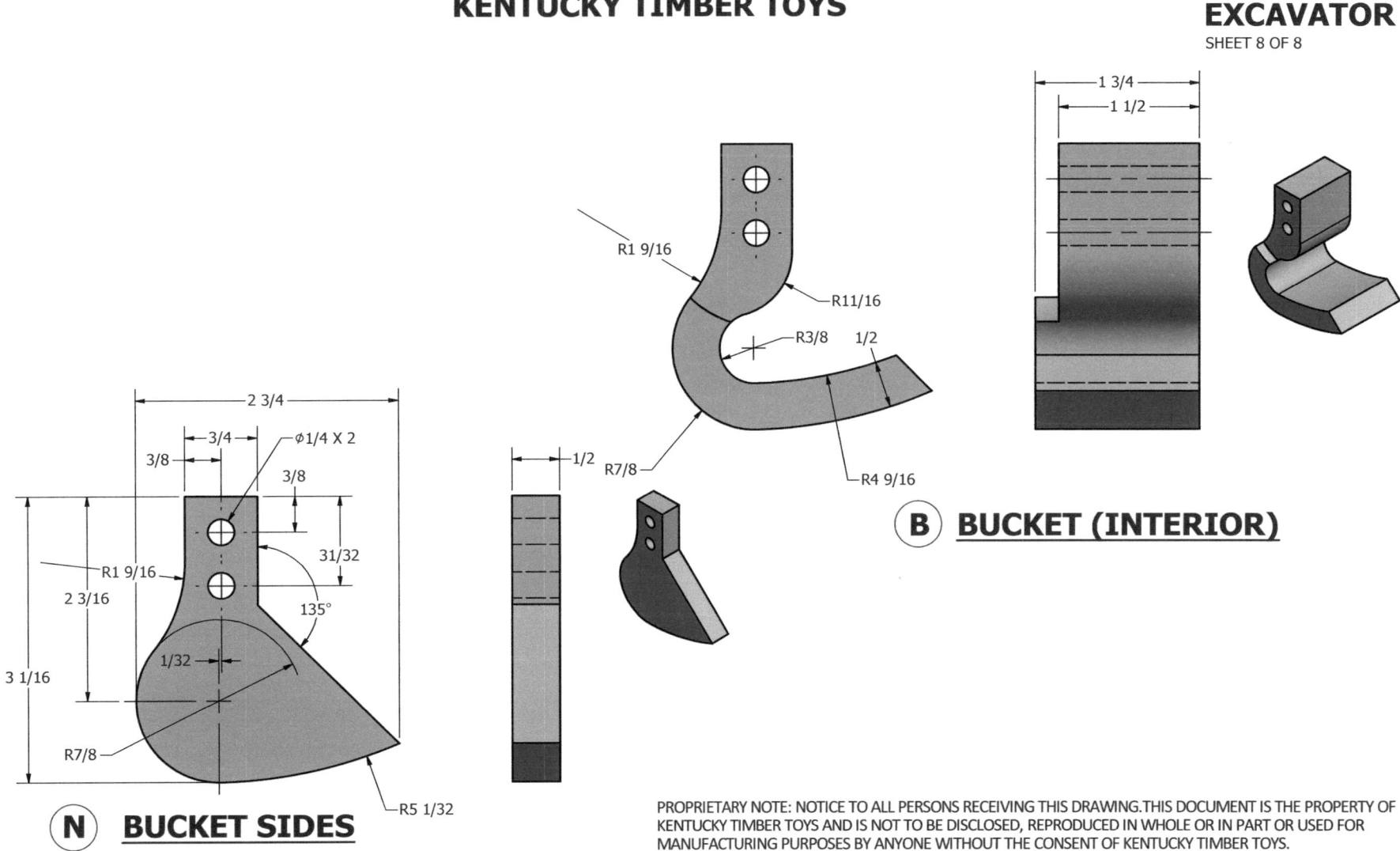

2 3/4

3/4

3/8

∅1/4 X 2

3/8

31/32

R1 9/16

2 3/16

135°

3 1/16

1/32

R7/8

R5 1/32

(N) BUCKET SIDES

1/2

R1 9/16

R11/16

R3/8

1/2

R7/8

R4 9/16

1 3/4

1 1/2

(B) BUCKET (INTERIOR)

THE KENTUCKY TIMBER FORKLIFT

The Forklift that you are about to build is a favorite of the children and teaches eye hand coordination that the parents love and actually loads and unloads the pallets, which the children love. We made ours 15 inches long, 6 ½ inches wide and 10 inches tall. It works with other toys that we have developed like the semi and flatbed trailer.

Tools Recommended:

Drill / Drill Press	Sander / Drum Sander/ Sand paper	Gorilla Wood Glue
Hammer / Mallet	¼ and 9/32 Drill bits	3 and 1 ¼ Día Hole Saw
Jig Saw / Band saw	(5) – 12" Clamps	¼" round over bit
Router	File or Wood Rasp	Flush cut trim saw

Materials Needed:

A piece of Douglas Fir 4 x 4 x 11 (This will make parts A, B, C and D)

Make sure you read, understand and follow all of the safety instructions that come with your power tools.

A piece of 2 x 6 x 20 white Pine (this will make parts E, F and the Cargo Blocks)

¼ Dowel Rod (comes in 48" lengths), this will make parts M and V)

3/8 Dowel Rod (comes in 48" lengths), this will make part N)

1 inch Dowel Rod (comes in 48" lengths), this will make part O)

1 x 4 x 8 white / yellow pine or poplar (this will make part J)

¼ x 4 x 36 white / yellow pine or poplar (this will make G, I, K, P, Q, R and S) and the pallets

1 ¼ Día Wooden Ball (This can be purchased at any hobby shop. Makes part L)

3/8 x 4 x 4 white / yellow pine (makes part H)

Layout:

The body (parts A, B, C and D) will all be laid out on one piece of Douglas Fir 4 x 4 x 12, the wheels and fenders (parts E and F) are cut from a 2 x 6 x 10 and finally the front fork assembly are all cut from Popular (see your material listing).

1)   Draw out the Body (part A), Cab (part B), Front Block and Wheel Hubs. We chose Douglas Fir for the color contrast, ease of shaping and sanding, cost containment and the finished appearance. When you get to cutting and drilling the parts it will be easier and safer to drill all your holes as indicated in the raw material prior to cutting them out. The larger block provides better stability and better clamping or hand hold surface area than the small cut out pieces. Now, drill your 1 ¼ inch Cab hole and the two 9/32 holes in your wheel hubs.

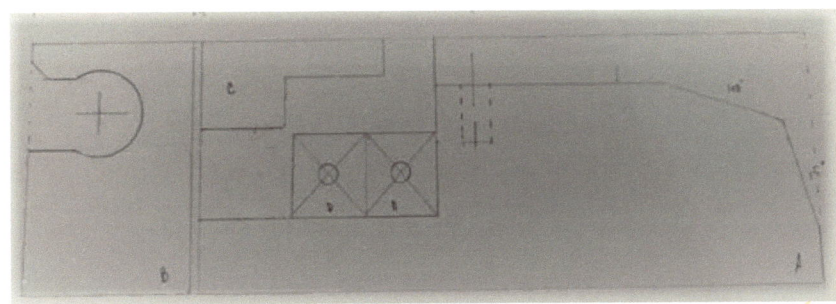

In drilling the 1 ¼ with a hole saw, it will not go all the way through. You will need to finish the cut out with the band saw or use a 1 ¼ Forstner Bit to dill all the way through. Finish cutting out all the other parts from the block. With this done you have completed phase 1 of the build.

Phase 2 starts with laying out the wheels and fenders on a 2 x 6 (parts E and F from the lower part of the 2 x 6). The upper three blocks will be used to make the cargo for the pallets at the end of the build.

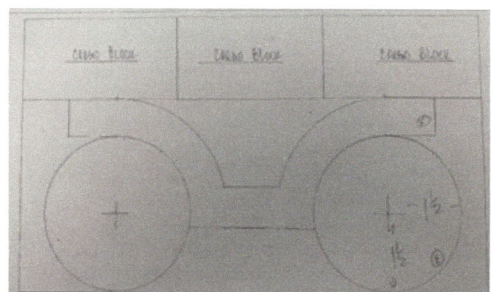
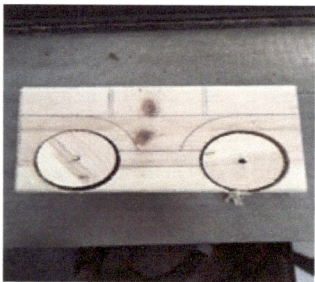

Drill you wheels out of the 2 x 6 (parts E) and then cut the cargo block section off and then cut out the fenders (part F). You should have what is shown. Repeat this process so that you have two fenders and four wheels.

Now sand all the parts to your preference. We routered all the parts to take all the sharp edges off. If you are not comfortable with a router just sand all the edges until smooth. We only routered one side of each fender so that the surface that is glued to the body is flat and provides the

Make sure you read, understand and follow all of the safety instructions that come with your power tools.

best adhesion. This will complete phase 1 and 2 of the build. Now that you are this far, let's begin assembling what you have done. Glue the body (parts A, B and C) together and clamp.

While this is drying, make you muffler with parts N and O (picture 1). Take the muffler (part O) and drill a 3/8-inch hole through the part. Slide the Muffler pipe (part N) through the hole and glue in place. You will want a ¼ inch exposed on the top of the muffler, then place into the muffler hole in the body (part A) that you drilled in the beginning. Space the muffler assembly a little shorter than the cab. This will make sure that does not get broken off or someone falls onto a sharp object.

Glue the fender spacer support (part T) fits in between the bottom of the fenders. This provides support and structure for the fenders. We used two flat long boards to apply even pressure to all fender sections. Next glue the Fenders (part F) onto the body (part A so that the tops of the fenders are even with the top of the front block and the lower part of the body (part A). You will notice that the lower section of the fenders hangs below the body in the center.

Then take the wheels (part E) and tap the Axles (Part M) into one of the wheels. This will be a press fit and no glue should be required. Slide the Wheel Hub (Part D) onto the other end of the Axle and tap the second wheel into place.

Center the wheel assemblies in the fenders and glue. You should have an assembly as shown below. Set that aside to dry. This is the end of Phase 2.

Start phase 3 of the build by cutting out the forks (part G) and the back plate (part H). Then cut out the main support plate (part J) and the Interactive Slide (part I), as shown below. On the Interactive slide save one of the two cut sections as one of them will become part K, the interactive Ball support.

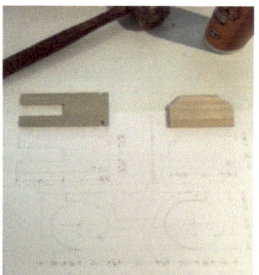  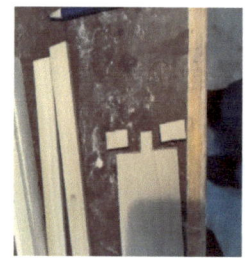

Cut out the two slide face plates (parts Q) and the slide space plates (parts R). Glue the Slide Space plates (part R) onto the front of the main support plate (part J), as shown in below.

Then glue the Fork Space plate (part S) centered on the fork back plate (part H) as shown. Finally take one of the small pieces (part K) that were cut from the interactive slide plate (part I) and glue it onto the ½ stem on part I.

Make sure you read, understand and follow all of the safety instructions that come with your power tools.

Once dry take the interactive slide (part J and now K) and round them over. This will be about a ½ dia so that the ball will fit snuggly onto it. Drill the interactive ball (part L) with a ½ inch hole and then glue into place. Before gluing the ball on we took and sanded a 45-degree angle on part K for aesthetic purposes only.

Glue the fork back plate and fork space plate (parts H and S) centered and flush with the bottom of the interactive slide plate.

Once dried it should fit into the main support plate (part J) and in between the slide space plates (part R) as shown below.

Now that the main slide support is dry (parts J and R) glue that assembly to the front of the forklift body. When dry, use a ¼ inch drill bit and drill 1-inch-deep holes into the face of the Forklift body using the main face plate as a guild. Using 1/4 x 1 ¼ inch dowel rod, tap them into the four holes with glue to secure everything together.

Make sure you read, understand and follow all of the safety instructions that come with your power tools.

Ok, let's now finish the fork assembly by gluing the forks (part G) to the bottom of the slide, slide spacer and fork back plate (parts H, I and S). Once dry, you should have a fork assembly that looks like center picture.

Fit and glue into place parts V and trim flush. You may need to run a file or a rasp in the groove to allow the slide to work properly.

Glue the slide face plates into place. Once dry the slide assembly should fit into place (You might have to fine tune the slide with a file or wood rasp). This leaves the last piece to put into place which is part P, the lift support plate. Congratulations you have finished the build.

Make sure you read, understand and follow all of the safety instructions that come with your power tools.

Now that you have completed this project, you will need to make some pallets with cargo so that the child you built this for can have something to load and unload. We used some ¼ x ½ x 4 stock along with some ½ x ½ x 4 stock. Glued them together and squared them on the belt sander. The cargo Blocks from the fender cut out, we rounded over to eliminate any sharp edges and glued them to the pallets (this way you don't have wooden blocks being left on the floor to be stepped on or being lost in the house. In this particular case the Semi and flatbed trailer is the toy that seems to get the most use with the forklift.

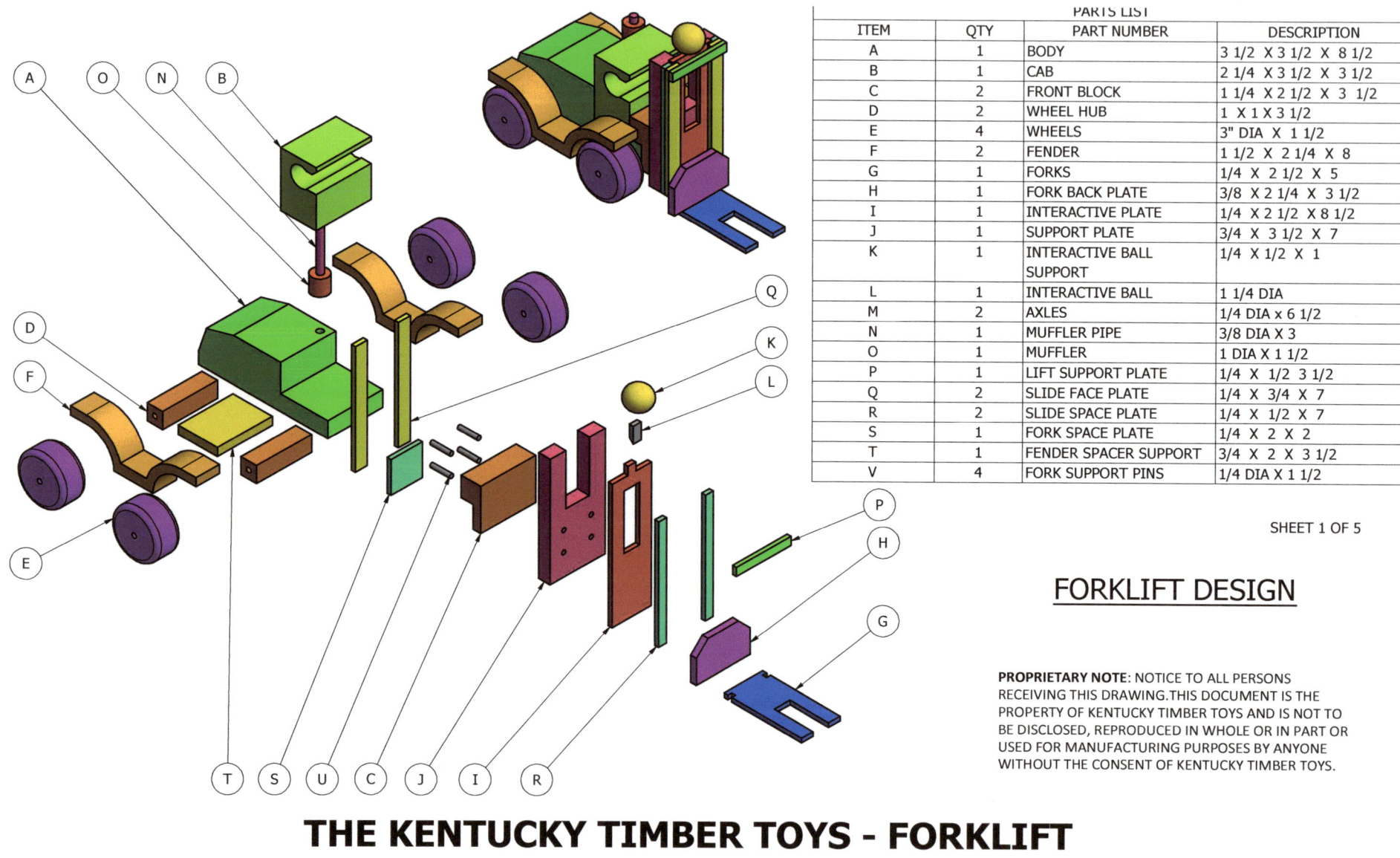

PARTS LIST

ITEM	QTY	PART NUMBER	DESCRIPTION
A	1	BODY	3 1/2 X 3 1/2 X 8 1/2
B	1	CAB	2 1/4 X 3 1/2 X 3 1/2
C	2	FRONT BLOCK	1 1/4 X 2 1/2 X 3 1/2
D	2	WHEEL HUB	1 X 1 X 3 1/2
E	4	WHEELS	3" DIA X 1 1/2
F	2	FENDER	1 1/2 X 2 1/4 X 8
G	1	FORKS	1/4 X 2 1/2 X 5
H	1	FORK BACK PLATE	3/8 X 2 1/4 X 3 1/2
I	1	INTERACTIVE PLATE	1/4 X 2 1/2 X 8 1/2
J	1	SUPPORT PLATE	3/4 X 3 1/2 X 7
K	1	INTERACTIVE BALL SUPPORT	1/4 X 1/2 X 1
L	1	INTERACTIVE BALL	1 1/4 DIA
M	2	AXLES	1/4 DIA x 6 1/2
N	1	MUFFLER PIPE	3/8 DIA X 3
O	1	MUFFLER	1 DIA X 1 1/2
P	1	LIFT SUPPORT PLATE	1/4 X 1/2 3 1/2
Q	2	SLIDE FACE PLATE	1/4 X 3/4 X 7
R	2	SLIDE SPACE PLATE	1/4 X 1/2 X 7
S	1	FORK SPACE PLATE	1/4 X 2 X 2
T	1	FENDER SPACER SUPPORT	3/4 X 2 X 3 1/2
V	4	FORK SUPPORT PINS	1/4 DIA X 1 1/2

SHEET 1 OF 5

FORKLIFT DESIGN

THE KENTUCKY TIMBER TOYS - FORKLIFT

Make sure you read, understand and follow all of the safety instructions that come with your power tools.

THE KENTUCKY TIMBER FORKLIFT

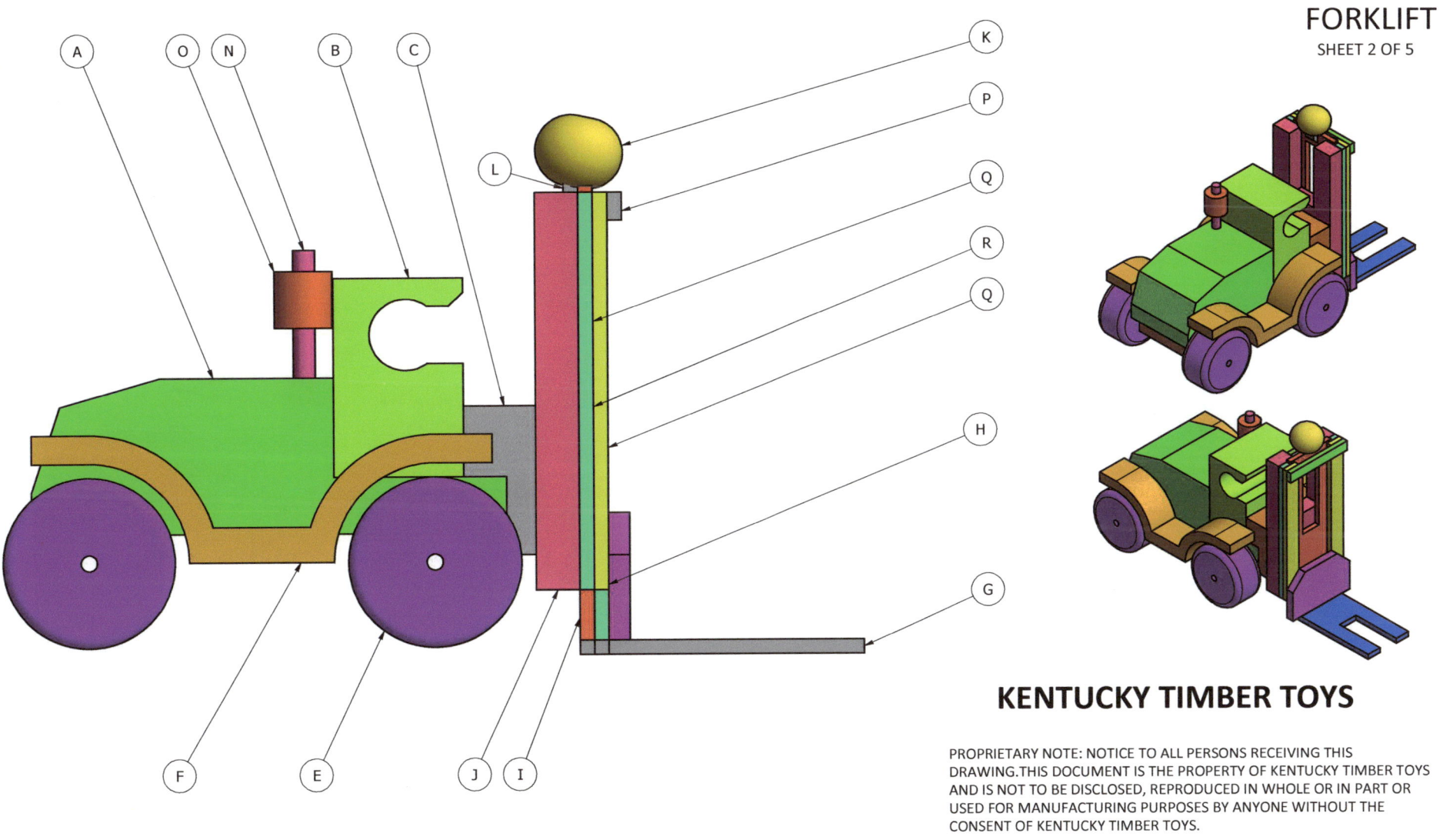

KENTUCKY TIMBER TOYS

Make sure you read, understand and follow all of the safety instructions that come with your power tools.

THE KENTUCKY TIMBER TOYS

FORKLIFT
SHEET 3 OF 5

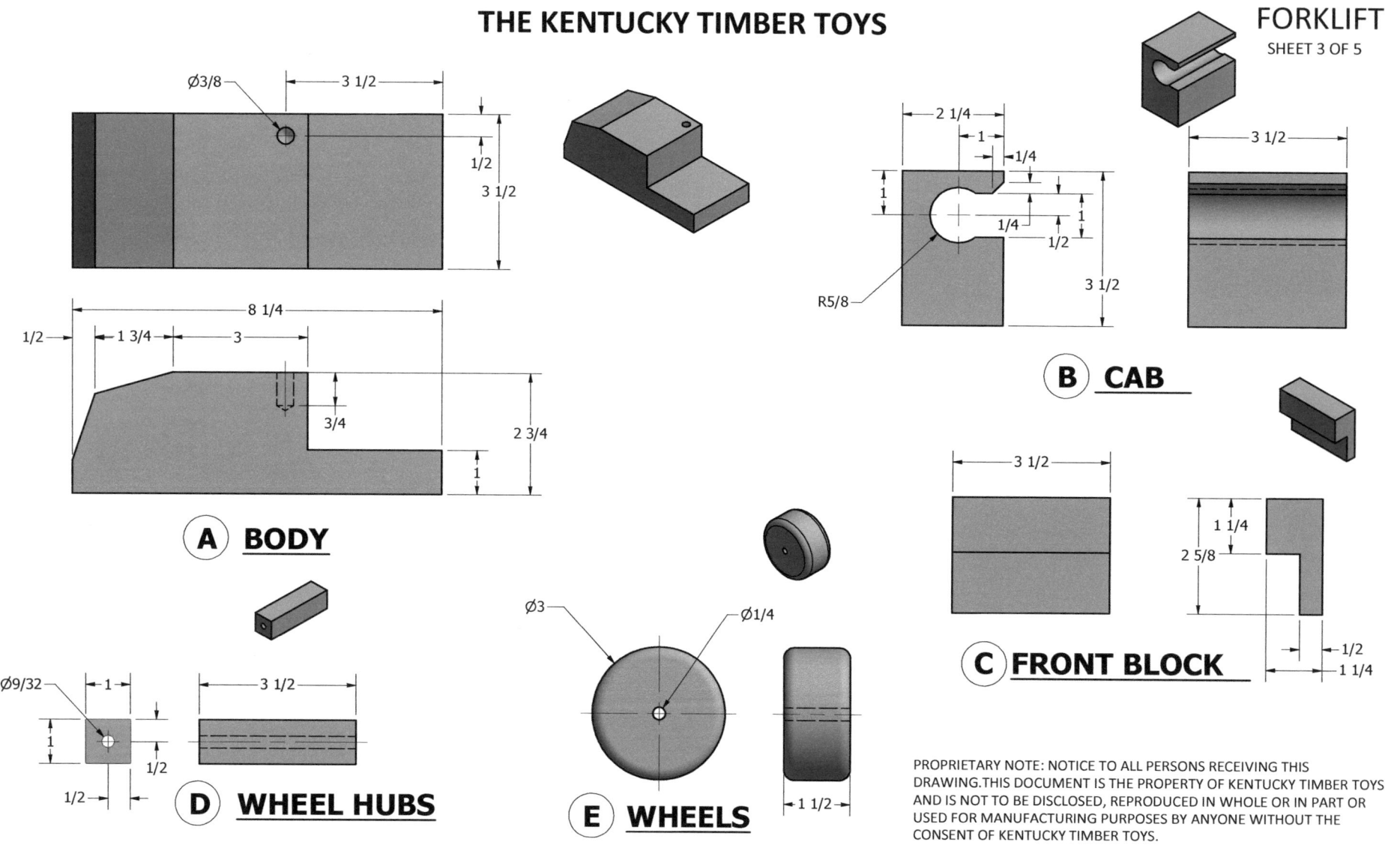

Ø3/8

3 1/2

1/2

3 1/2

8 1/4

1/2

1 3/4

3

3/4

2 3/4

1

A) BODY

2 1/4

1

1/4

1

1/4

1/2

1

3 1/2

R5/8

3 1/2

B) CAB

3 1/2

1 1/4

2 5/8

1/2

1 1/4

C) FRONT BLOCK

Ø9/32

1

1

1/2

1/2

3 1/2

D) WHEEL HUBS

Ø3

Ø1/4

1 1/2

E) WHEELS

Make sure you read, understand and follow all of the safety instructions that come with your power tools.

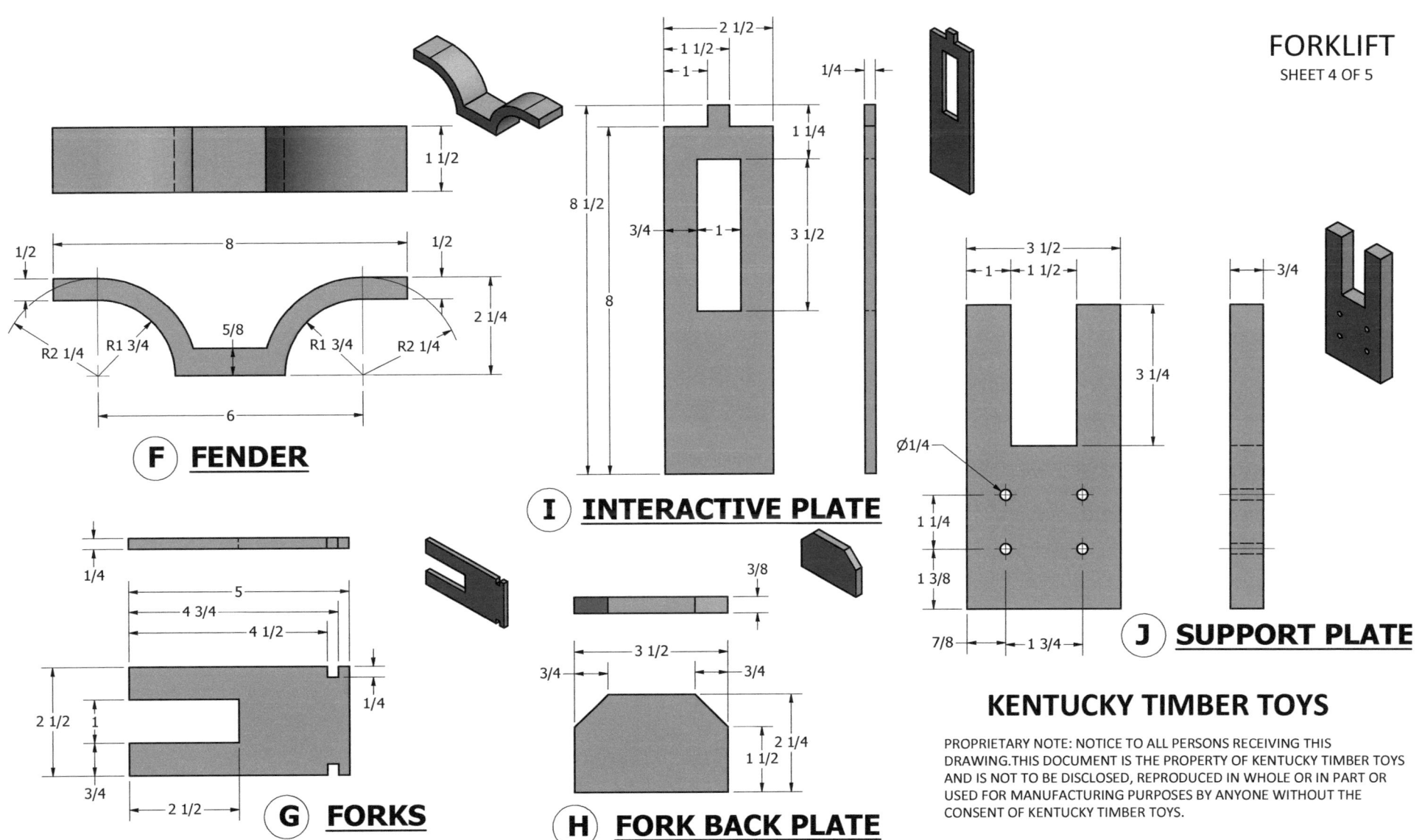

FORKLIFT
SHEET 4 OF 5

F **FENDER**

I **INTERACTIVE PLATE**

G **FORKS**

H **FORK BACK PLATE**

J **SUPPORT PLATE**

KENTUCKY TIMBER TOYS

Make sure you read, understand and follow all of the safety instructions that come with your power tools.

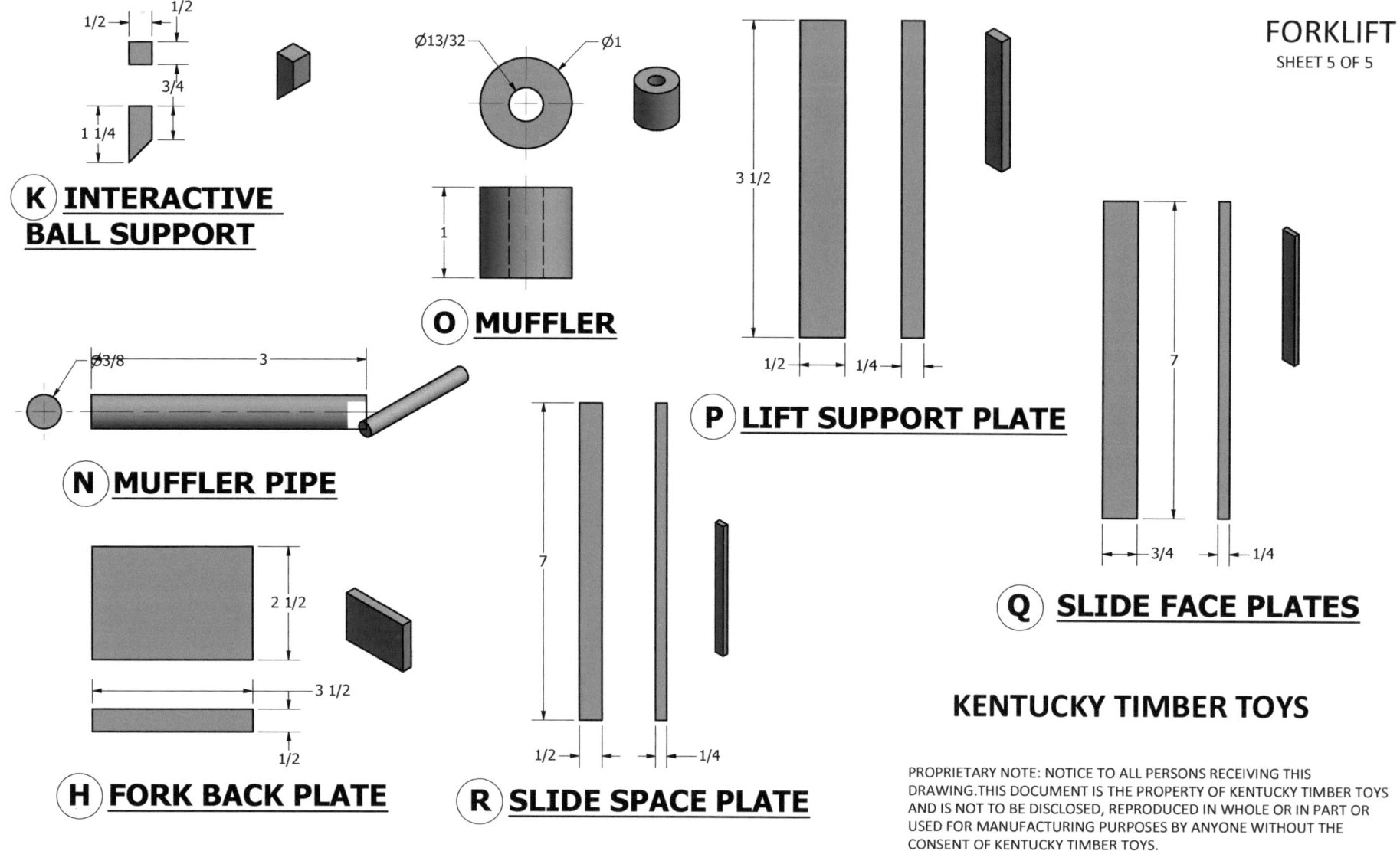

FORKLIFT
SHEET 5 OF 5

1/2 1/2
3/4
1 1/4

K **INTERACTIVE BALL SUPPORT**

Ø13/32 Ø1
1

O **MUFFLER**

3 1/2
1/2 1/4

P **LIFT SUPPORT PLATE**

Ø3/8 3

N **MUFFLER PIPE**

2 1/2
3 1/2
1/2

H **FORK BACK PLATE**

7
1/2 1/4

R **SLIDE SPACE PLATE**

7
3/4 1/4

Q **SLIDE FACE PLATES**

KENTUCKY TIMBER TOYS

PROPRIETARY NOTE: NOTICE TO ALL PERSONS RECEIVING THIS DRAWING.THIS DOCUMENT IS THE PROPERTY OF KENTUCKY TIMBER TOYS AND IS NOT TO BE DISCLOSED, REPRODUCED IN WHOLE OR IN PART OR USED FOR MANUFACTURING PURPOSES BY ANYONE WITHOUT THE CONSENT OF KENTUCKY TIMBER TOYS.

Make sure you read, understand and follow all of the safety instructions that come with your power tools.

THE KENTUCKY TIMBER TOY BOX

The Kentucky Timber Toy Box is not a small toy box, it actually folds out into your Childs own small toy store. All of our toys fit on the shelves and floor area so that your child can walk right into the middle of the toy box and select what he or she wants and does not have to bend over and dig through toys piled in a heap.

You will not have to worry about the lid falling down on them because the lid folds back onto itself. There also is a soft foam spacer that fits in-between the draw bridge door and the floor so that your child does not trip or fall, because the heal of their shoe grabs.

Recommended Tools Needed:

Table Saw / Radial Arm Saw with Dado set	Chop Saw / radial arm saw with single blade	Router with ¾ straight bit
6- Four foot clamps	6- Eight foot clamps	Raised Panel Cutter with router table
½ inch chisel	belt sander / orbital sander	Hammer / mallet
Screw Driver (Phillips)	24 spring clamps	Drill with 1/8 bit
2 Large Feather Boards	Combination Square	#2 Pencils
Counter Sink Drill bit	Flush Trim Hand Saw	Wood screw pilot bit

Materials Needed:

10	2 x 4 x 8 ft pine or Douglas fir (depends on the color contrast that you may want)
3	1 x 12 x 72 edge glued finger joint boards
4	1 x 16 x 72 edge glued finger joint boards
1	Small box of #6 X 1 ¼ wood screws
1	3/8 dowel rod. (Comes in 36 – 48 inch lengths)
1	Bottle of wood glue (We used Gorilla wood glue)
2	3" Barrel locks
5	4 "Gate Hinges
1	poly styrene water pipe wrapping (black in color)

The first thing that you will need to do is square and flatten all the 2 x 4's that you have purchased. Standard milling on all pieces to ensure that everything was the same thickness and all faces were square before starting is the first step. Depending on the time of year the recommendation is to do this step this first thing in the morning, so that when it is done, the parts can be laid out and cut. All 2 x 4 sections as provided on the diagrams should be done prior to assembly. If freshly milled pieces sit for any length of time they will twist and problems will arise when putting the frames together.

Glue the frames together and clamped them making sure everything is square as the frames are assembled. There was a great number of large clamps used for this project.

Kentucky Timber Toy Box

Now that the frames are completed, choose the best-looking sides of each frame and have them face outwards. Lay that side against the table top or work station that is being used. Now take the router with the 3/4" straight bit and ball bearing and router each interior frame ½ in deep.

This will form the rabbit that will accept the raised panels that will be made later. Remember to square the corners of each small frame with a sharp chisel, because the raised panels will not fit unless you do.

In the next step, select which large frame section will be the front, back and sides and lay them out accordingly. With the same router bit, you will need to set you depth to ¾ inches and run the router down both the sides of the two side frames. You will need to do this in several passes because you are making a rabbit ¾ inch deep and 1 ½ inches wide. This will allow you to now accept the front and back frames into the side frames. Another way of doing this is to place a dado set into a table saw and run the sections through that. You will still need to do several passes because most Dado sets will only stack to ¾ of an inch wide. You will also dado the bottom of each large panel with a ¾ inch dado so that the floor can be put into place.

Once that process is completed you can now make the raised panels. Use a raised panel cutter in the router table and go very slowly. Several passes will be necessary to get the final results. Use feather boards to keep the stock flush against the vertical back splash of the router table.

Once all the panels are done you should be able to fit them into the inner small frames and glue them into place.

Once dry, remove the clamps and then, because this project will contain screws and hardware, screw each section together on the lap joints that have been created and sink the head of the screws ¼ inch deep so that you can go back and plug the screw heads with dowel rod. Let that dry, trim the dowel rods flat and then sand all the surfaces down. You should have a box that looks like this:

Now lay the box on its back and on the center panel rails draw a pencil line down the middle of each rail and across the bottom. You will need a circular saw to carefully cut the lines out on the sides and plunge cut the bottom to create the drawbridge door. You will need to hand saw the remains of what the circular saw left to break the draw bridge door free.

To begin to attach the hardware and finish the toy box, the placement of the door hinges and the barrel locks will be the first step. Squaring the top in place and marking your hinge placement will be the next step.

The recommendation is to use a hand chisel for this operation to make sure your cuts are exact and that you mark and pre drill all your hole first before attaching them with screws. This will ensure a tight fit and that you do not split the wood when attaching the hinges. Once you have the hinges secured. Square the top on the box (you should have a ¾ inch overhang on all sides of the box) and then on the back half of top you will measure in the ¾ of an inch (for the overhang and then another ¾ of an inch to center yourself on the 1 ½ back frame.

Mark both ends of the top in this fashion and draw a straight line. This will mark your center line and every 6 inches you will indicate the placement of a screw on it. Pre-drill the holes with a wood screw pilot bit and sink the head of the screws ¼ inch deep so that you can go back and plug the screw heads with dowel rod. Let that dry, trim the dowel rods flat and then sanded all the surfaces down. Now it is a matter of fitting in your shelving on both sides of the door and then placing in the 2 x 4 x 24 flooring and then finally the ¾ inch band that fits around the bottom lip of the top on the box. Congratulations, you have just completed the toy box build. When the door is open, place the poly styrene water pipe wrapping in the space between the door and the floor of the toy box. This will make a soft transition into the box and will keep anyone from closing the door if a child is inside.

KENTUCKY TIMBER TOYS

PARTS LIST			
ITEM	QTY	PART NUMBER	DESCRIPTION
A	14	UP RIGHTS FOR THE BOX	1 1/2 X 3 1/2 X 28
B	4	CROSS MEMBERS (SIDES)	1 1/2 X 3 1/2 X 27
C	4	CROSS MEMBERS (FRONT AND BACK)	1 1/2 X 3 1/2 X 48
D	4	SIDE PANELS	3/4 X 10 X 24
E	4	FRONT / BACK SIDE PANELS	3/4 X 12 X 24
F	2	FRONT /BACK CENTER PANELS	3/4 X 12 X 24
G	2	SIDE SHELVES	3/4 X 12 X 24
H	1	BOTTOM	3/4 X 26 X 49
I	2	TOP	3/4 X 14 1/4 X 51
J	2	TOP BANDING (FRONT/ BACK)	3/4 X 3/4 X 51
K	4	TOP BANDING (SIDES)	3/4 X 3/4 X 14 1/4
L	5	HINGES (SILVER/GOLD)	4" HINGE
M	2	BARREL LOCKS (SILVER/GOLD)	3" BARREL LOCKS
N	4	RAISE ENTRY FLOOR	2 X 4 24

TOY BOX
SHEET 1 OF 3

Make sure you read, understand and follow all of the safety instructions that come with your power tools.

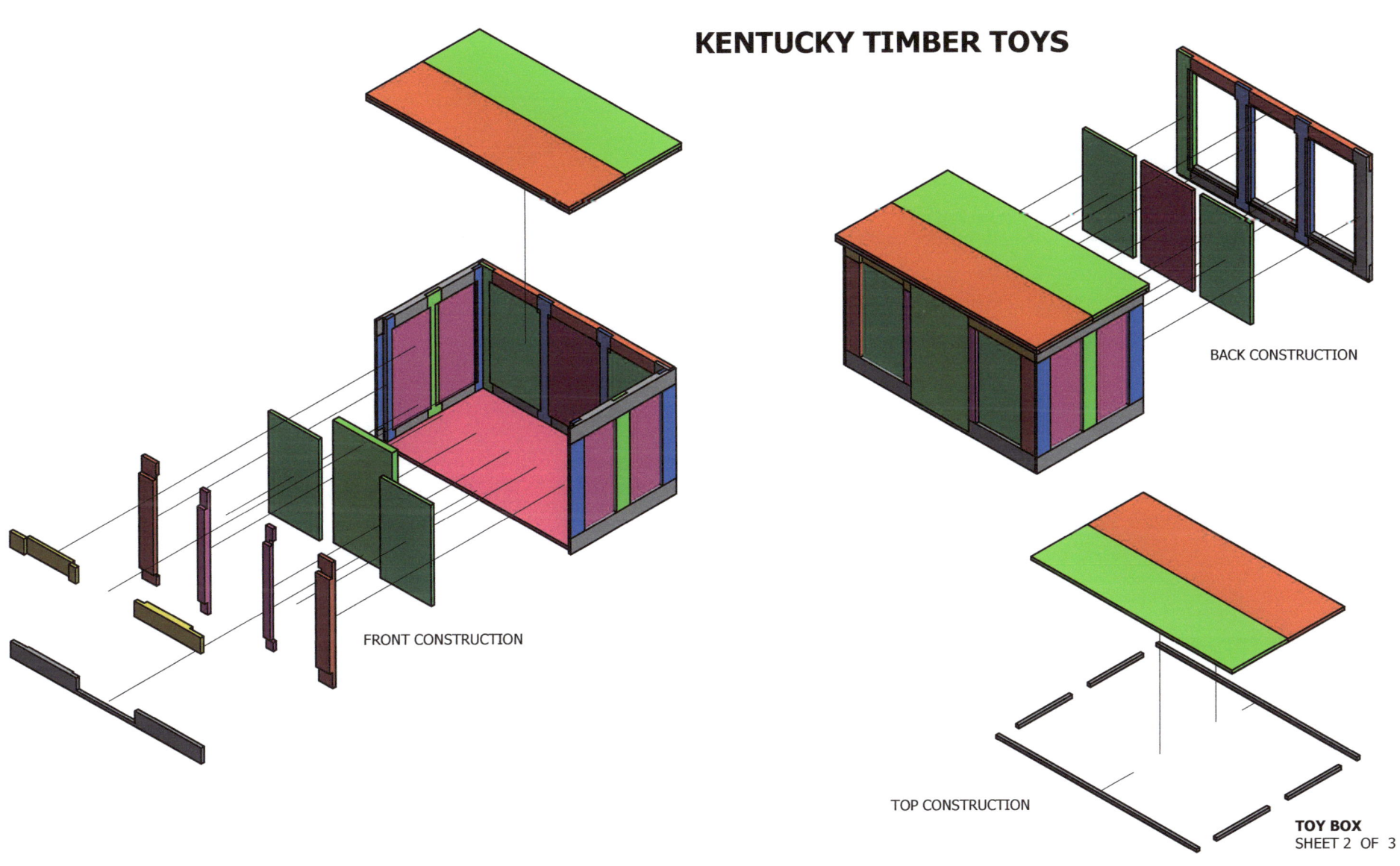

KENTUCKY TIMBER TOYS

BACK CONSTRUCTION

FRONT CONSTRUCTION

TOP CONSTRUCTION

TOY BOX
SHEET 2 OF 3

Make sure you read, understand and follow all of the safety instructions that come with your power tools.

KENTUCKY TIMBER TOYS

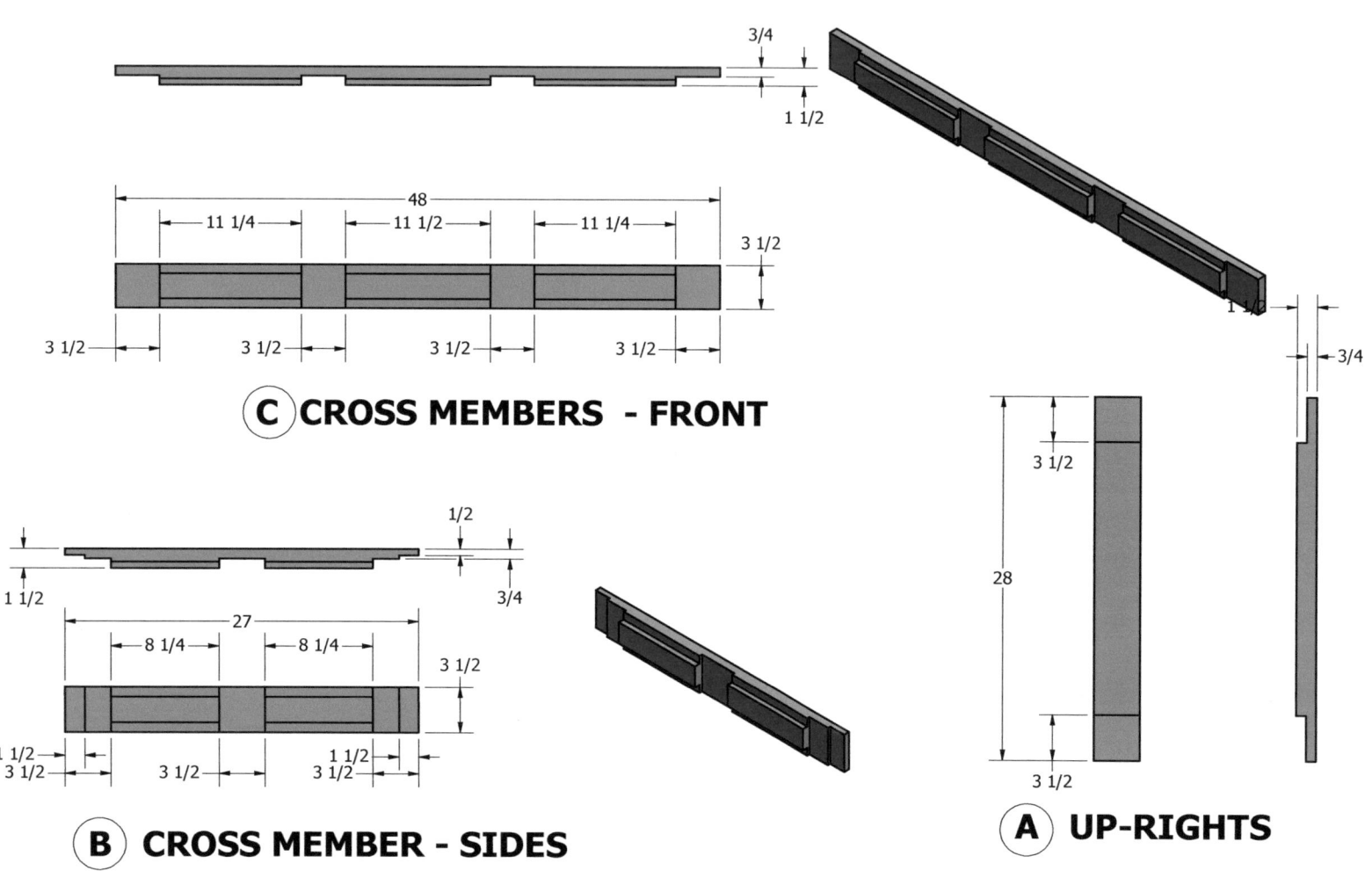

3/4

1 1/2

48

11 1/4   11 1/2   11 1/4

3 1/2

3 1/2   3 1/2   3 1/2   3 1/2

Ⓒ CROSS MEMBERS - FRONT

1/2

1 1/2

3/4

27

8 1/4   8 1/4

3 1/2

1 1/2
3 1/2   3 1/2   1 1/2
3 1/2

Ⓑ CROSS MEMBER - SIDES

3/4

3 1/2

28

3 1/2

Ⓐ UP-RIGHTS

TOY BOX
SHEET 3 OF 3

Make sure you read, understand and follow all of the safety instructions that come with your power tools.

www.ingramcontent.com/pod-product-compliance
Lightning Source LLC
Chambersburg PA
CBHW040816120626

46551CB00004B/569